MERCHANTS IN PLENTY

Joseph Smyth's Belfast Directories

of
1807 and 1808

WITH AN HISTORICAL INTRODUCTION AND BIBLIOGRAPHY
OF BELFAST DIRECTORIES TO 1900
BY

J.R.R.ADAMS

D1477093

ULSTER HISTORICAL FOUNDATION

606896

Published 1991
by the Ulster Historical Foundation
12 College Square East
Belfast
BT1 6DD
Northern Ireland

All rights reserved. No part of this publication may be reproduced,
stored in a retrieval system or transmitted in any form or by any means,
electronic, mechanical or otherwise without the prior permission of the
publisher.

© 1992 Ulster Historical Foundation

ISBN 0 901905 49 6

Printed by Graham & Sons (Printers) Ltd
51 Gortin Road
Omagh
Co. Tyrone
Northern Ireland

This book has received support from the Cultural Traditions Programme
of the Community Relations Council which aims to encourage
acceptance and understanding of cultural diversity.

The Ulster Historical Foundation wishes to thank the Governors and
Librarian of the Linenhall Library for permission to reproduce the
original directories.

Illustrations are reproduced courtesy of the Ulster Folk and Transport
Museum.

Cover Design by Wendy Dunbar

CONTENTS

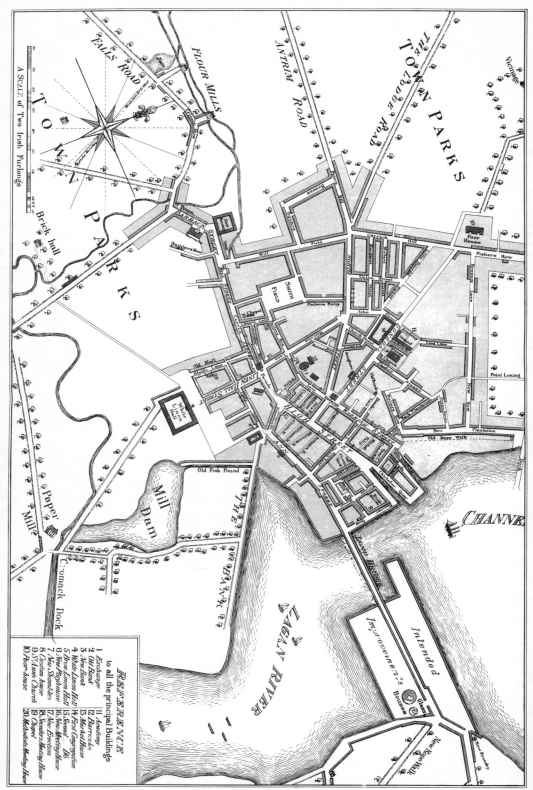

Belfast in 1791. Population, 18,320.

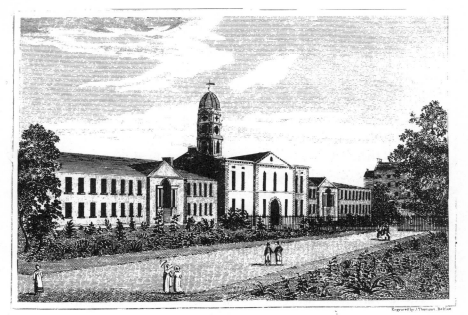

THE WHITE LINEN HALL

PREFACE

On Thursday, August 21st, 1806, Sir Richard Colt Hoare visited Belfast during the course of his tour of Ireland. He was not particularly impressed, and his comments were brief.

> 'On descending this mountain, Belfast soon opens; the fields white with linen, the country bespread by numerous manufactories; in short, a commercial air enlivens the whole scenery. We found excellent accomodations at Wilson's hotel.
>
> 'The town of Belfast has more attractions to the merchant than to the antiquary: it has some good streets, but no public buildings particularly worthy of remark; the houses are in general built with brick, and the roofs covered with slate.'

But while Sir Richard recognised the general air of bustling

1

commerce in Belfast, his stay was far too short for him to become aware that Belfast at this time was rather more than just another substantial country town.

The population, it is true, was not large by modern standards. According to a census carried out by Arthur Thomson in 1807, the total population was 22,095, of whom 7,213 were males over the age of ten, and there were 3,514 inhabited houses. The town was dominated by cotton, the manufacture of which had by then displaced linen. Of 678 looms in the town, only four wove linen, and some 2,100 people were employed in the cotton trade in the town, many more in the surrounding area. There were large spinning mills. The McCracken mill alone had 14,000 spindles and employed two hundred people.

Commerce abounded and throve in other areas as well. The foundations were being laid of such later important industries as engineering and shipbuilding. There was a fairly large publishing trade. Despite the monopoly of the cotton business, Belfast was an important linen trade centre, thanks to the considerable manufacture in the rest of the province – as Sir Richard saw, the surrounding areas were covered in bleach greens. There were two newspapers. Sixty-seven vessels were registered at the port of Belfast. This was the Belfast that Sir Richard Colt Hoare saw. But there was another Belfast.

This was the Belfast that liked to think of itself as the 'Northern Athens'. Such still thriving societies as the Society for Promoting Knowledge [Linen Hall Library] and the Literary Society were in full swing. The growth of intellectual Belfast as well as commercial Belfast is shown by the fact that in the two years covered by these directories the Galvanic Society, the Society for Acquiring Knowledge, the Medical Library and the Belfast Classical and Commercial School were founded, the Belfast Monthly

Magazine was started and plans were afoot for a Harp School and the Belfast Academical Institute.

Communications with other parts of Ireland were becoming easier as well. The Northern Mail Coach had a daily service between Belfast and Dublin, the trip taking twenty-one hours (with a double guard to ensure the passenger's safety); at Newry there was a connecting service to Dungannon. Within Belfast itself there was a rudimentary taxi service in the form of sedan chairs – a reminder that Belfast stood between two eras.

It was against this background that the first directory published in Belfast was launched, by the firm of Smyth & Lyons. They had been publishing a substantial almanac since 1803, and the idea of publishing a directory as well must have occurred to them in 1805. Belfast had now 'arrived' as a substantial Irish town with a large trade, and a directory was required – Dublin had had one since 1751. They announced in December 1805 that the first issue would come out in January 1806. Materials were collected, and indeed it must have got as far as proof stage, as the volume containing this unique series of directories in the Linen Hall Library (which originally belonged to Joseph Smyth, one of the printers) has the torn-up fragments bound in. Probably Smyth & Lyons were dissatisfied by the completeness. In any case the project was postponed until the following year.

The 1807 directory came out in January of that year, attached to the almanac, priced at two shillings and eightpence halfpenny. This was announced as 'the first attempt in the north of Ireland', confirming the non-publication of the 1806 issue. The 1807 issue was a success, and Smyth & Lyons, by the end of January, were announcing a reprint, to be sold separately from the almanac for the convenience of visiting businessmen.

The 1808 directory followed this pattern, but for some reason no directory was published for 1809, and indeed this was the end of directory publishing in Belfast for a decade. These little directories are consequently an important and unique source for Belfast history and genealogy.

Directories, however useful a source, need to be treated with caution nevertheless. For one thing, they are not a complete listing of the population. The directories for 1807-8, for instance, cover only the names of businessmen in the town. Each businessman would have employed a varying number of people from two or three up to hundreds, and these names do not appear, nor do those of their families.

Directories, again are only a good as their compilers make them. Information can be gathered carelessly, and changes not noticed until years after they have occurred. In the case of the Smyth & Lyons directories, these problems would not have been serious. Belfast, though a large town, was still small enough for virtually every businessman and tradesman to know each other: errors were likely to be minimal. It is therefore fitting that these unique and almost unknown first directories published in Belfast should see the light of day again.

CHRONOLOGICAL
LIST
OF
BELFAST DIRECTORIES,
1805–1900

THE PAPER MAKER

HOLDEN'S TRIENNIAL DIRECTORY. 4th. ed. London: Holden, 1805.
[Typescript copies of Belfast entry in Belfast libraries].

BELFAST DIRECTORY, FOR 1806. Belfast: Smyth & Lyons, [1806].
[Linen Hall Library, unique fragments].

BELFAST DIRECTORY, FOR 1807. Belfast: Smyth & Lyons, [1807].

BELFAST DIRECTORY, FOR 1808. Belfast: Smyth & Lyons, [1808].

HOLDEN'S TRIENNIAL DIRECTORY. 5th. ed. London: Holden, 1809.
[Typescript copies of Belfast entry in Belfast libraries].

Bradshaw, Thomas. BELFAST GENERAL & COMMERCIAL
DIRECTORY FOR 1819; . . . WITH A DIRECTORY AND HISTORY OF
LISBURN. Belfast: Finlay, 1819.

SMYTH'S DIRECTORY TO BELFAST AND ITS VICINITY. Belfast:
Smyth, 1819.

COMMERCIAL DIRECTORY OF IRELAND, SCOTLAND, . . . FOR
1820–21 & 22. Manchester: Pigot, 1820.

PIGOT AND CO.'S OF DUBLIN AND HIBERNIAN PROVINCIAL
DIRECTORY. Manchester: Pigot, 1824.

BELFAST DIRECTORY FOR 1831–2. Belfast: Donaldson, [1831].

MATIER'S BELFAST DIRECTORY, FOR 1835–6. Belfast: Matier, 1835.

MARTIN'S BELFAST DIRECTORY, FOR 1839. Belfast: Martin, 1839.

MARTIN'S BELFAST DIRECTORY, FOR 1840–41. Belfast: Martin
1840.

MARTIN'S BELFAST DIRECTORY, FOR 1841–42. Belfast: Martin,
1841.

MARTIN'S BELFAST DIRECTORY, FOR 1842–3. Belfast: Martin,
1842.

POST-OFFICE BELFAST ANNUAL DIRECTORY FOR 1843–44. Belfast:
Wilson, 1843.

HENDERSON'S NEW BELFAST DIRECTORY, . . . FOR 1843–44.
Belfast: Henderson, 1843.

HENDERSON'S BELFAST DIRECTORY, . . . 1846–47. Belfast:
Henderson, 1846.

I. SLATER'S NATIONAL COMMERCIAL DIRECTORY OF IRELAND.
Manchester: Slater, 1846.

HENDERSON'S BELFAST DIRECTORY. Belfast: Henderson, 1850.

HENDERSON'S BELFAST DIRECTORY. Belfast: Henderson, 1852.

BELFAST AND PROVINCE OF ULSTER DIRECTORY FOR 1852. Vol. 1.
Belfast: Henderson, 1852.

BELFAST AND PROVINCE OF ULSTER DIRECTORY. Vol. 2. Belfast:
Henderson, 1854.

BELFAST AND PROVINCE OF ULSTER DIRECTORY FOR 1856. Vol. 3.
Belfast: Henderson, 1856.

SLATER'S . . . ROYAL NATIONAL COMMERCIAL DIRECTORY OF
IRELAND. Manchester: Slater, 1856.

BELFAST AND PROVINCE OF ULSTER DIRECTORY FOR 1858–9.
Vol. 4. Belfast: Henderson, 1858.

ADAIR'S BELFAST DIRECTORY FOR 1860–61. Belfast: Adair, 1860.

BELFAST AND PROVINCE OF ULSTER DIRECTORY FOR 1861–62.
Vol. 5. Belfast: Henderson, 1861.

BELFAST AND PROVINCE OF ULSTER DIRECTORY FOR 1863–64.
Vol. 6. Belfast: Henderson, 1863.

BELFAST AND PROVINCE OF ULSTER DIRECTORY FOR 1865–66.
Vol. 7. Belfast: [News-letter], 1865.

BUSINESS DIRECTORY OF BELFAST AND PRINCIPAL TOWNS IN THE
PROVINCE OF ULSTER, FOR 1865–66. Belfast: Wynne, 1865.

BELFAST AND PROVINCE OF ULSTER DIRECTORY FOR 1868. Vol. 8.
Belfast: [News-letter], 1868.

BELFAST AND PROVINCE OF ULSTER POST-OFFICE DIRECTORY, . . .
1870. Vol. 1. Belfast: News-letter, 1870.

SLATER'S . . . ROYAL NATIONAL COMMERCIAL DIRECTORY OF
IRELAND. Manchester: Slater, 1870.

BELFAST AND PROVINCE OF ULSTER DIRECTORY FOR 1877. Vol. 9.
Belfast: News-letter, 1877.

BELFAST AND DISTRICT DIRECTORY, AND ULSTER GUIDE, FOR
1878. London: Brookes and Thompson, [1878].

BELFAST AND PROVINCE OF ULSTER DIRECTORY FOR 1880. Vol. 10. Belfast: News-letter, 1880.

SLATER'S ROYAL NATIONAL COMMERCIAL DIRECTORY OF IRELAND. Manchester: Slater, 1881.

BELFAST AND PROVINCE OF ULSTER DIRECTORY FOR 1884. Vol. 11. Belfast: News-letter, 1884.

BELFAST DIRECTORY FOR 1887. Vol. 12. Belfast: News-letter, 1887.

BELFAST AND PROVINCE OF ULSTER DIRECTORY FOR 1890. Vol. 13. Belfast: News-letter, 1890.

BELFAST AND PROVINCE OF ULSTER DIRECTORY FOR 1892. Vol. 14. Belfast: News-letter, 1892.

CLARKE'S BELFAST AND NORTHERN COUNTIES DIRECTORY. Glasgow: Clarke, [1893].

BELFAST AND PROVINCE OF ULSTER DIRECTORY FOR 1894. Vol. 15. Belfast: Newsletter, 1894.

SLATER'S ROYAL NATIONAL COMMERCIAL DIRECTORY OF BELFAST AND ITS SUBURBS. London: Kelly, 1894.

BELFAST AND PROVINCE OF ULSTER DIRECTORY FOR 1895. Vol. 16. Belfast: News-letter, 1895.

BELFAST AND PROVINCE OF ULSTER DIRECTORY FOR 1896. Vol. 17. Belfast: News-letter, 1896.

BELFAST AND PROVINCE OF ULSTER DIRECTORY FOR 1897. Vol. 18. Belfast: News-letter, 1897.

BELFAST AND PROVINCE OF ULSTER DIRECTORY FOR 1898. Vol. 19. Belfast: News-letter, 1898.

BELFAST AND PROVINCE OF ULSTER DIRECTORY FOR 1899. Vol. 20. Belfast: Newsletter, 1899.

BELFAST AND DISTRICT TRADES' DIRECTORY . . . 1899. Edinburgh: Town & County Directories Ltd., [1899].

BELFAST AND PROVINCE OF ULSTER DIRECTORY FOR 1900. Vol. 21. Belfast: News-letter, 1900.

BELFAST AND DISTRICT TRADES' DIRECTORY . . . 1900. Edinburgh: Town & County Directories Ltd.,]1900].

BELFAST

DIRECTORY,

FOR 1807;

OR,

A LIST OF THE NAMES AND PLACES

OF

THE MERCHANTS TRADERS, &c.

Alphabetically arranged;

ALSO THE PRINCIPAL PROFESSIONAL CHARACTERS.

To be published Annually.

PRINTED AND PUBLISHED BY SMYTH & LYONS,
High-street.

BELFAST DIRECTORY;

FOR, 1807.

MERCHANTS, TRADERS, &c.

A

ADAIR, Simon, cooper, 51, Waring-street

Agnew, James, ladies' shoemaker, 19, Skipper's-lane

Alexander, John, & co. merchants, Belfast-mills

Alexander, Samuel, tanner, 78, North-street

Alexander, John, carman's-inn-keeper, 11, Peter's hill

Alexander, John, junior, & co. cotton spinners, and manufacturers, cotton court, Waring-street

Allen, Ann & Mary, haberdashers and milliners, 16, Castle-street

Allen, Mary Ann, haberdasher, 10, Cornmarket

Allen, William, boot and shoemaker, High-street

Anderson, Drummond, printer of the Commercial Chronicle, Wilson's-court

Anderson, James, watch and clockmaker, 2, Waring-street

Andrews, Samuel, merchant-tailor, 7, Marlbro'-street

Appleton, David, hosier, 38, High-street

Archer, Samuel, bookseller, 22, High street

Armstrong, John, breeches-maker, 53, Castle-street

13

Armstrong, Robert, cotton-manufacturer, 40, Smithfield

Ashmore, John and Richard, merchants, 54, Waring-street

Atkinson, Eliza, haberdasher, 59, High-street

Atkins, John, coach and house painter, 27, Prince's-street.

B

Bailie, Robert, merchant, 1, Upper Chichester-street

Bailie, James, merchant, 185, North-street

Bailie, John, boot and shoemaker, 32, Ann-street

Bailie, Robert, hat manufacturer, 5, Bridge-street

Bailie, John, auctioneer, 28, Castle-street

Baird, James, confectioner, 11, Rosemary-lane

Baker, James, muslin manufacturer, 32, North-street

Bancroft, Robert, dyer, 2, Mill-field

Barkley, James, tavern and ordinary-keeper, 3, Sugar-house-entry

Barnett, Andrew John, merchant, High-street

Barnett, John, tanner, 41, Castle-street

Barr, Alexander, woollen-draper, 75, High-street

Batt, Narcissus & Robert, merchants, Calendar-street

Becket, Oliver, grocer,& spirit dealer,31,Rosemary-lane

Belfast porter brewry, 22, Smith-field

Bell, John & co. muslin manufacturers, Margaret-street

Bell, John, brewer, 51, Hercules-lane

Bell & Kennedy, wholesale printed calico, and linen-warehouse, 62, Waring-street

Bell & Haughton, hardware merchants, High-street

Bell, William, woollendraper, 20, Bridge-street

Bell, Alexander, woollendraper, 2, Bridge-street

Bell, Isaac, senior, upholsterer, 60, High-street

Bell, Isaac, junior, upholsterer, Bank-buildings

Bell, William, dyer, 8, Mill-field

Bell, Francis, bookbinder, 73, High-street

Bell, John, pawnbroker, 28, Smith-field

Bell & Harvey, nursery and seedsmen, 15, Church-lane

Bentley, George, machine maker, 35, Smith-field

Berwick, William & co. merchants, 1, North-street

Bigger, David, merchant, 5, High-street

Birnie, Clotworthy, ship broker, and auctioneer, 1, Chichester-quay

Black, Matthew, woollendraper, 7, Bridge-street

Black, Alexander, grocer, 24, High-street

Blackader, John, boot & shoemaker, 20, North-street

Blackwell, William James, wholesale haberdasher, 1, Donegall-street

Blackwell, William, cabinet-maker, 46, Donegall-street

Blackwood, Charles, victualler, 20, Corn-market

Blackwell, Alexander, linendraper, 39, High-street

Boomer, James, cotton spinner and manufacturer, 18, Mill-street

Blow, Ward, & co. paper manufacturers, 97, Ann-street

Boswell, John, watchmaker, 87, Ann-street

Burdot, John Baptist, ladies' and gentlemen's hair-dresser and perfumer, Castle-street

Bowden, James, soap-boiler and tallow-chandler, 61, Ann-street

Boyce, William, grocer, 95, Ann-street

Bradford, James, merchant, 7, Store-lane

Bradford, George & Benjamin, merchants, High-street

B 2

Boyd, Nathaniel, tavern-keeper, 34, Berry-street

Broadley, Ben. & co. cotton wool and tow card manufacturers, 20, Smithfield

Brown, David, painter and glazier, 53, Mill-street

Brown, John, last-maker, 7, Berry-street

Brown, John, anchor-smith, 10, Marlbro'-street

Brown, John, patten and ladies' shoemaker, 62, Hercules-lane

Brown, Samuel, merchant, Calendar-street

Brown, Samuel, hairdresser and perfumer, 7, Castle-street

Bryson, John, grocer, 93, Ann-street

Bullen, John, nursery and seedsman, 101, Ann-street

Buchannan, Walter, merchant, 4, Chichester-quay

Burke, Robert, feather and skin merchant, 28, Hercules-lane

Burke, Patrick, feather warehouse, 17, Skippers-lane

Burns, William, merchant-tailor, 10, Bridge-street

Burns, Robert, hairdresser and peruke maker, 16, Skipper's-lane

Burnside, John, furniture cotton warehouse, 15, Donegall-street

Byers, William & co. muslin manufacturers, 21, Donegall-street.

C

Callwell, Robert, merchant, Upper Chichester-street

Campbell, Samuel & James, merchants, 192, North-street

Campbell, Hugh, muslin manufacturer, 12, Brown-street

Campbell, Christopher, inn and livery stable keeper, 90, Ann-street

Campbell, Charles, boot and shoemaker, 10, Mill-street

Campbell, William, rope and twine manufacturer, 40, North-street

Campbell, Michael, stone, and marble yard, 23, Waring street

Carmichael, Robert, woollendrapei, 9, High-street

Carrol, William victualler, 30, Ann-street

Carson, James, grocer, spirit and wine merchant, 1 & 2, Cornmarket

Carson, James, timber merchant, 39, Ann-street

Carson, Thomas, breeches-maker, 61, Castle-street

Carson, William, fustian warehouse, 5, Hercules-lane

Caughey, Isabella, slop-shop, 10, Chichester-quay

Caughey, Mary, ship chandlery shop, High-street

Caulfield, John, seedsman, 171, North-street

Cavan, John, grocer, 2, High-street

Chambers, Brice & co. wine and spirit merchants, 9, Ann-street

Christian, Thomas, cart-maker, 9, Marlbro'-street

Clarke, Sampson, hat manufacturer, 8, Castle-street

Clarke, John, cabinet maker, 17, Rosemary-lane

Clawson & Hill, grocers and tobacconists, 28, Rosemary-lane

Cleland, Jane, china, glass and staffordshire warehouse, 12, Castle-street

Coats, Victor, founder, and starch manufacturer, Lagan, Ballymacarret

Cochran, George, fancy furniture ware-room, 10, Smith-field

Cochran, Ernest, tailor, 1, Wilson's-court

Colville, James, woollendraper, 14, Bridge-street

Colville, John, woollendraper, 21, Bridge-street

Cooney, John, victualler, Cornmarket

Cooper, John, grocer, High-street

Cowan, Jane & Ellen, grocers, 81, Ann-street

Craig, Samuel, wine and spirit merchant, 4, Marlbro'-street

Crawford, Hugh, merchant, 26, Donegall-street

Crawford, Walter, iron merchant, 10, Donegall-street

Crawford, Ann, grocer, 16, Church-lane

Crawford, James, cabinet-maker, 18, Waring-street

Crossen, James, calico manufacturer, 14, Brown-street

Crossen, Wm. & James, muslin manufacturers, Brown-street

Cuddy, John, glazier, paint, oil and glass store, 25, Church-lane

Cumming, Mary, haberdasher, 31, Bridge-street

Cummin, Samuel, leather seller, 163, North-street

Cunningham, John, merchant, 52, High-street

Cunningham, John & Thomas, brewers and spirit merchants, 36, Castle-street

Cunningham, John, hosier, 13, Donegall-street.

D

Daniel, Stephen, dyer, 34, North-street

Davis, Robert, merchant, 11, Chichester-quay

Davis, Joy, hat manufacturer, 26, Bridge-street

Davis, Robert, glazier, paint, oil and glass store, 19, North-street

Davison, Gawn, grocer and tobacconist, 74, Ann-street

Davison, William, merchant, 63, High-street

Davison, John, haberdasher, 4, Bridge-street

Dawson, William, boot and shoemaker, High-street

Delap, Robert, broker, 6, Chichester-quay

Demsey, Matthew, pawnbroker, 4, Pottinger's entry

Dickson, Simon, boot and shoemaker, 21, North-street

Dickson, William, cotton manufacturer, 24, Waring-street

Doherty, John, printer and bookseller, 33, Bridge-street

Doherty, Patrick, tavern and ordinary-keeper, Gregg's-entry

Doherty, Edward, Spirit dealer, 83, Ann-street

Donaldson, Jane, haberdasher, 67, High-street

Donaldson, John, block-maker, and pump-boarer, High-street

Donelly, Daniel, spirit dealer, 48, High-street

Dornan, John, glazier, 18, Church-lane

Douglass, William & co. merchants, 5, Marlbro'-street

Drummond, Isabella, circulating library, 10, Castle-street

Duffield, Samuel carman's-inn-keeper, 111, North-street

Dunlop, James & Robert, coal-factors, Prince's-street

Dyke, R. W. crayon and miniature painter, and drawing master, 64, Mill-street.

E

Edwards, Benjamin & Sons, glass manufacturers and founders, Ballymacarret

Ekenhead, Thomas, rope and twine manufacturer, 46, Ann-street

Elliot, John, linen merchant, 11, Donegall-street

English, Thomas, dyer, 12, Mill-field.

F

Fallon, Francis, grocer and spirit dealer, 23, Church-lane

Faloon, James, Spirit dealer and tavern-keeper, 2, Hanover-quay

Ferguson, R. & E. haberdashers, 81, High-street

Ferguson and Elliot, wine and spirit merchants, 55, Hercules-lane

Fetherston, Ann, and sisters, haberdashers, 27, Castle-street

Finlay, Robert, cotton spinner and manufacturer, 15 Mill-field

Finlay, Alexander, soap-boiler and tallow-chandler, High-street

Finlay, Usher, slop-shop, High-street

Fitzsimons, Alice, haberdasher, 76, High-street

Fitz-imons, James, tailor, 72, High-street

Fitzsimons, Richard, tailor, 54, Ann-street

Fletcher, Thomas, soap-boiler and tallow-chandler, 145, North-street

Forcade, John, saddler, 56, Castle-street

Frazier, Joseph, grocer, 12, Patrick-street

Frazier, James, carman's-inn-keeper, 72, Peter's-hill

Freebairn, John, stocking-frame maker, 65, Patrick-street

Fulton, Nathan, soap-boiler and tallow-chandler, 3, North-street

Fulton, James, tavern and stable keeper, 13, Hercules-lane.

G

Gamble, Robert, merchant, 196, North-street

Gamble, Arthur, merchant, 17, North-street

Gardner, Henry, L. watchmaker and dentist, 27, High-street

Gardner, John, gun-smith, 10, Rosemary-lane

Gardner, Arthur, grocer, High-street

Geddes, M'Dowell & co. Belfast glassworks, 79, Peter's-hill

Gemmill, Robert, muslin manufacturer, 50, Donegall-street

Getty, Robert, merchant, 16, North-street

Getty, John, cabinetmaker, 48, Donegall-street

Gibson, Samuel, merchant, 20, Donegall-street

Gibson, Samuel & co. brewers, 181, North-street

Gibson & Simms, haberdashers, Donegall-street

Gihon, Jane, haberdasher, 5, Castle-street

Gillet, Henry, tavern-keeper, Belfast hotel, 22, Arthur-street

Gillies, John, merchant, 5, Custom-house-quay

Gilmore, Joseph, baker, 12, Ann-street

Glancey, James, stay-maker, 21, Rosemary-lane

Gold, John, bookbinder, mustard-street

Gordon, Robert & Alexander, merchants, 6, High-street

Gordon, John, grocer, 197, North-street

Gordon, James, muslin manufacturer, 15, Brown-street

Gowdy, James, hairdresser, 173, North-street

Graham, Campbell, wine and spirit merchant, 100, Ann-street

Graham, Hugh, linen draper, 5, Peter's-hill

Graham, Thomas, copper and tin-smith, High-street

Graham, John, block-maker and pump-borer, High-street

Grainger, James, bricklayer, 84, Ann-street

Grainger, John, grocer, 85, Ann-street

Grainger, William, baker, 25, Mill-street

Gray, John, hosier, 47, High-street

Gray, William, boot and shoemaker, High-street

Greenlaw, Robert, merchant, Church-street

Greer, James, boot and shoemaker, 8, Corn-market

Greer, Samuel, grocer, 189, North-street

Greer, William, senior, weavers' mechanic, 64, North-street

Greer, William, junior, weavers' mechanic, 113, North-street

Greg & Blacker, merchants, Ann-street

Greg & Boyd, vitriol works, Ballymacarret

Grimmer, Conrad, confectioner, 53, Castle-street

Grogan, John, linen-merchant, Donegall-square

Grogan, Robert, linen-merchant, Henry-ville

Groves, David, glover and skinner, 23, Castle-street

Groves, William, glover and skinner, 35, Church-lane.

H

Hadskis, Ann, grocer, 194, North-street

Hall, John Joshua, watchmaker, 64, Donegall-street

Hamilton, Robert, tailor, 18, Wilson's-court

Hamilton, John, cork-cutter, 112, Hercules-lane

Hannay, M'William, & co. cotton yarn warehouse, 53, Donegall-street

Hamill, Ann, grocer, 53, High-street

Hanratty, James, soap-boiler and tallow chandler, 62, Ann street

Harper, James, master joiner, 23, Mill-street

Harrison, Mary, haberdasher, 29, Bridge-street

Hart, Robert, glazier, 33, Church-lane

Haslett & Montgomery, coast brokers, 8, Chichester-quay

Hay, Robert, watchmaker, 176, North-street

Henan, Hugh, umbrella-maker, 88, Ann-street

Henderson, Robert, joiner, 74, Brown-street

Henesey, David, sen. fancy-chairmaker, 12, Rosemary-lane

Henesey, George, fancy chair maker, 13, Rosemary-lane

Heron, Thomas, merchant, Ann-street

Herdman, Gibson & co. brewers, Ann-street

Herdman, James, tanner and currier, 9, Mill-street

Hewett, Samuel, wine and spirit merchant, 24, Ann-street

Hibner, Ellis, victualler, South-William-street

Higgins, John machine maker, 102, Mill-field

Higginson, Wm. grocer and spirit dealer, 41, North-street

Hill, Edward, grocer, 193, North-street

Hodgins, Thomas, saddler, 2, Hercules-lane

Hodgins, Thomas, saddler, 1, Rosemary-lane

Hodgson, Robert & John, booksellers, 4, High-street

Hoey, Samuel, cooper, 69, Hercules-lane

Holmes & Barklie, merchants, 8, Ann-street

Horner, Anthony, muslin manufacturer, 16, Smith-field

How, John & Thomas, muslin manufacturers, Church-street

Huddleston, Francis & co. muslin manufacturers, 6, Pottinger's-entry

Hudson, Christopher, tanner, 138, North-street

Huggard, George, soap-boiler, and tallow-chandler, 7, Mill-street

Hughes, Thomas & James, grocer, 168, North-street

Hughes, Thomas, grocer, 8, North-street

Hughes, Ann, haberdashery and toyshop, 33, Rosemary-lane

Hughes, Thomas, conveyancer, 52, Waring-srreet

23

Hunter, William, grocer, 2, Donegall-street

Hutton, William, hardware and toyshop, High-street

Hyndman, Robert, snuff and tobacco manufacturer, 78, High-street.

J

Jack, Samuel, victualler, 147, North-street

Jamison, William, inn-keeper, 28, North-street

Jamison, James, tanner, 95, North-street

Janson, Henry, M. painter and glazier, 48, Waring-street

Johnson & Fisher, wholesale woollendrapers, 34, Rosemary-lane

Johnson, William & co. wholesale woollendrapers, and haberdashers, 70, Donegall-street

Johnson & Halliday, wholesale woollendrapers and haberdashers, 70, Donegall-street

Johnson, Young & co. wholesale haberdashery warehouse, 15, Waring-street

Johnston, Richard, grocer, 77, North-street

Johnston, William, baker, 16, Mill-street

Johnston, Robert, haberdasher, 21, Mill-street

Johnston, James, grocer and spirit merchant, 184, North-street

Jordan, Simon, cabinet maker, 29, Smith-field

Joy, Holmes, & Tomb, merchants, Wine-cellar-entry

Joy, Henry, paper manufacturer, Pottinger's-entry

Joy, James, and co. cotton manufacturers, 3, Wine-cellar-entry

Joyce, Charles Valentine, & co. wine and spirit merchants, 3, Waring-street

Ireland, Frances, haberdasher, 89, High-street

Ireland, M. & E. haberdashers, 88, High-street

Ireland, John, livery stables, 87, High-street

Ireland, Thomas, cotton spinner and manufacturer, 19, Mill-field

Irwin, William, cooper, 28, Waring-street.

K

Kearney, John, china and delf seller, 66, Ann-street

Kearns, Hugh, spirit dealer, 64, Ann-street

Kelso, Paul, grocer and spirit dealer, 166, North-street

Keenan, John, painter and glazier, 29, Berry-street

Kennedy, James Trail & co. merchants, Leg's-lane

Kennedy, John, junior, merchant, Waring-street

Kennedy, John, baker, 79, Hercules-lane

Kennedy, Sarah, haberdasher, 61, High-street

Kennedy, Alexander, woollendraper, 6, Bridge-street

Kennedy, Patrick, baker, 14, Church-lane

Kennedy, Daniel, cutler, 19, Chapel-lane

Kennedy, Charles, grocer, 195, North-street

Kenning, Thomas, muslin warehouse, 21, Castle-street

Kerr, Daniel, tavern-keeper and ordinary, 92, Ann-street

Kilbee, Hannah, haberdasher, 57, High-street

Kilbee, James, & co. Old Sugar House, 3, Rosemary-lane

Kirker, James, tanner and currier, 45, North-street

Kirkpatrick, John, merchant, 51, Waring-street

Kirkpatrick, Samuel, grocer, 24, Church-lane

Kirkpatrick, Thomas, soap-boiler and tallow-chandler 44, High-street

Knox, John, watch maker, 15, High-street

Knox, John, boot and shoemaker, 36, High-street.

L

Lamont, Ann, earthen-ware shop, 8, Skipper's-lane

Langtry, George, merchant, 20, Waring-street

Law, James, baker, 50, High-street

Law, Samuel, tanner, 104, North-street

Law, James, tanner, 102, North-street

Law, Andrew, brazier, 10, Hercules-lane

Lawrence, James, perfumer and hairdresser, 101, Ann-street

Leathem, Robert, linen merchant, 69, Donegall-street

Leathem, Robert, confectioner, 58, Waring-street

Lepper, George, watchmaker, 9, Bridge-street

Lepper, Francis, watchmaker and dentist, 59, Castle-street

Lepper, Charles, grocer and spirit merchant, 192, North-street

Lewes, Robert, boot and shoemaker, 29, High-street

Lindsay, Edward, nursery and seedsman, 4, Donegall-street

Linn, Cath. haberdasher and milliner, 2, Castle-street

Linn, Patrick, inn-keeper, white cross, 1, Castle-street

Linn, Robert & co. soap-boilers and tallow-chandlers, High-street

Linn, David, spirit dealer, 122, Barrack-street

Littlewood, John, wholesale cotton yarn, woollen and hosiery warehouse, Waring-street

Luke, John & son, woollendrapers, 34, Bridge-street

Luke, James, pottery-shop, 200, North-street

Lyle & Riddle, hardware merchants, 64, High-street

Lynn, Jane, haberdasher, 80, High-street

M

Magee, William, bookseller and stationer, 25, Bridge-street

Magee, James, tavern and stable keeper, 60, Ann-street

Maphet, William & co. salt works, Ballymacarret

Marshall, Hugh, tailor, Pottinger's-entry

Martin, Jane, tavern and stable keeper, 30, North-street

Martin, Thomas, baker, 26, Prince's-street

Martin, John & co. merchants, 11, Church-lane

Martin, George, hardware merchant, 28, Bridge-street

Martin, William & James, saddlers and curriers, 31, Castle-street

Martins & Park, merchants, 11, Church-lane

Matthews, James & Robert, merchants, 57, Ann-street

Matthews, John & Robert, boot and shoemakers, 8, Castle-street

May, Richard, grocer, wine and spirit merchant, 79, Ann-street

Meneally, James, grocer, 120, Barrack-street

Milford, John & co. cotton manufacturers and spinners, Winetavern-street

Millar, Mary, haberdasher, 84, Ann-street

Miller, James, auctioneer, Pottinger's-entry

Miller, George, rope and twine manufacturer, 153, North-street

Miller, Samuel, starch manufacturer, and provision merchant, Donegall-street

Miniss, Charles, peruke maker, 37, Ann-street

Mollyneaux, Joseph, baker and starch manufacturer, 34, North-street

Montgomeries, Staples & co. merchants, 2, Calender-street

Montgomery, Josias, saddler, 84, High-street

Montgomery, Gawn, wollendraper, 45, High-street

Montgomery, Ellen, haberdasher, 80, Ann-street

Montgomery, Henry, haberdasher, 13, Bridge-street

Montgomery, John, grocer, 24, Prince's-street

Montgomery, Tennent & co. New Sugar House, 8, Waring-street

Mooney, William, surveyor and measurer, 36, Hercules-lane

Moore, Stevenson, B. grocer, 11, Ann-street

Moore, Thomas, rope and twine manufacturer, High-street

Moor, Eliza, haberdasher, 30, North-street

Moreland, Arthur, victualler, 15, Cornmarket

Morgan, John, grocer, 141, North-street

Morrow, Samuel, grocer, 71, Ann-street

Mountford, Hugh, smith, 73, Ann-street

Mountford, John, cotton spinner and manufacturer, York-street

Muckle, Robert, wool and tow card maker, 165, North-street

Mulholland, Roger, architect, 12, Castle-street

Mulrea, William, woollendraper, 18, Bridge-street

Munfoad, James, salt refiner, 40, Waring-street

Munfoad, E. & M. haberdashers, 61, High-street

Murdoch, George, hearth and window-tax collector, 4, Chichester-quay

Murdoch, Richard, smith, 91, Ann-street

Murphy, Thomas, grocer, 14, Ann-street

Murray, Henry, grocer, 19, Church-lane

Murray, Timothy soap-boiler and tallow-chandler, 172, North-street

28

Mussenden, Charles, boot and shoemaker, 36, Ann-street

Myers, George, china, glass and earthen warehouse, 42, High-street.

Mc

Mackay, Alexander, editor of the Belfast News-Letter, 11, Bridge-street, and 19, Joy's-entry

M'Adam, James, hardware merchant, 69, High-street

M'Adam, George, hardware merchant, 70, High-street,

M'Auley & Kenley, haberdashers, 60, Castle-street

M'Burney, James, tailor, 35, Park's-entry

M'Bride, Ursula, haberdasher, 13, High-street

M'Bride, John, grocer, 167, North-street

M'Cabe, Edmond & Thomas, gilders and chair-makers, 59, Talbot-street

M'Cammon, John, tanner and currier, 44, Mill-street

M'Cappin, William, provision merchant, Cotton-court, Waring-street

M'Cartney, James, smith, 3, Marlbro'-street

M'Clarnon, Pat. provision merchant, 13, Hercules-lane

M'Clean, Adam, woollendraper, 68, High-street

M'Clean, Samuel & Andrew, wine and spirit merchants, 1, Sugar-house-entry

M'Clean, William, wine and spirit merchant, 188, North-street

M'Clean, Charles, silk dyer, 5, mill-street

M'Cleery, James, merchant, 187, North-street

M'Clement, David, grocer, 68, Ann-street

M'Clure, Bailie & Whitla, merchants, Donegall-quay

M'Clure, William, merchant, 8, Donegall-street

M'Clure, John, grocer, 119, Barrack-street

M'Clure, Robert, boot and shoemaker, 27, North-street

M'Clure, Joseph, boot and shoemaker, 43, North-street

M'Comb, Thomas, muslin and calico seller, 27, Church-lane

M'Comb, Thomas, timber merchant, 44, Waring-street

M'Connell, John, merchant, 9, Ann-street

M'Connell, Alexander, earthenware-house, High-street

M'Connell, William, farming-utensil-maker, 3, Smith-field

M'Cosh & Irwin, merchants, 7, Rosemary-lane

M'Cord, Andrew, grocer, 33, Rosemary-lane

M'Coubery, Robert, grocer, 93, Ann-street

M'Cracken, Margaret & co. muslin manufacturers, 30, Rosemary-lane

M'Cracken, R. Ann, haberdasher, 29, Castle-street

M'Cracken, John & co. cotton spinners, Donegall-street

M'Cracken, Francis, merchant, 30, Rosemary-lane

M'Crackens & co. rope and sail manufacturers, Fore-plantation

M'Cracken, William, cotton manufacturer, 29, Castle-street

M'Credie, John, saddler, 35, Castle-street

M'Creary, Mary, milliner, 9, Castle-street

M'Crum, John, fustian, cotton, and muslin manufacturer, 12, Skipper's-lane

M'Culloch, John, linen merchant, 150, North-street

M'Cully, William, publican and stable keeper, 20, Ann-street

M'Cune, Samuel, sea-bread baker, 7, Cow lane

M'Donnell, Thomas, merchant, 11, North-street

M'Fadden, Archibald, baker, 10, Ann-street

M'Garragh, Alexander, grocer, 65, Ann-street

M'Gibbon, John & co. wine and spirit merchants, 11, Waring-street

M'Ilroy, Archibald, muslin manufacturer, 16, Patrick-street

M'Kean James, grocer, 15, Ann-street

M'Kee, William, woollendraper, 1, Bridge-street

M'Kee, Robert, confectioner, 28, Ann-street

M'Kibbin, Hugh & co. tanners and glue manufacturers, 19, Mill-street

M'Kibbin, Beck, & co. wholesale haberdashers, 69, Waring-street

M'Lister, John, soap-boiler and tallow-chandler, 1, Ann-street

M'Main, Samuel, woollendraper, 16, High-street

M'Master, James, merchant, 38, North-street

M'Mullan, John, tavern keeper, 2, Pottinger's-entry

M'Neice, William, reed-maker, 6, Peter's-hill

M'Pherson, James, peruke maker and hair dresser, 44, Church-lane

M'Queelin, J. Davys, spirit dealer and tavern keeper, 9, Chichester-quay

M'Tier, James, baker, 76, North-street

M'Whinney, Thomas, grocer, 56, Ann-street

M'Whirter, James, grocer, 90, High-street

M'William, John & co. cotton-yarn warehouse, 53, Donegall-street.

N

Nagle, Francis, spirit merchant 12, North-street

Napier, William, brewer, 24, Back-of-the-river

Neill, Robert, watchmaker, 1, High-street

Neilson, Ann, haberdasher, 56, High-street

Neilson, William, watchmaker, 201, North-street

Newsam, William, tobacco and snuff manufacturer, 101, Ann-street

Newsam, William & co. wholesale haberdashers, 6, Donegall-street

Nicholl, Andrew, boot and shoemaker, 6, Church-lane

Nicholl, William, cooper, 3 Skipper's-lane.

O

O'Neill, Thomas, & co. printed calico, muslin and cotton-yarn warehouse, 66, Donegall-street

Orr, James, merchant, South-parade.

P

Palmer, John, spirit dealer and tavern keeper, 3, Hanover quay

Park, James, saddler, 182, North-street

Park, James, fustian and cotton manufacturer, 10, West-street

Parker, John, stone cutter, 11, Smith-field

Parkison, John, boot and shoemaker, High-street

Patrick, Hugh, baker, 8, Berry-street

Patterson, Robert & John, hardware merchants, 24, High-street

Patterson, Joseph, brick-layer, 51, Ann-street

Patton & M'Alister, factors, White-linen-hall....office, Calender-street

Patton, Isaac, wholesale haberdasher, 82, High-street

Patton, Frances, haberdasher, 18, High-street

Patton, Barbara, haberdasher, 79, High-street

Pinkerton, Andrew, merchant, 24, Bridge-street

Porter, Edward, cutler, 21, Corn-market

Potter, Mary, grocer, 25, Prince's-street.

Q

Quinn, Arthur, boot and shoemaker, 6, High-street

Quaille, Roger, inn, and stable-keeper 26, Prince's-street

R

Radcliff & Munce, wholesale woollendrapers, 3, Bridge-street

Radcliff & Black, calico and cotton yarn manufacturers, 1, Union-street

Ramsey, Esther, grocer, 20, Castle-street

Rea, John, merchant-tailor, 28, High-street

Reid Thomas, spirit merchant, 2, Leg's-lane

Reid, William, plumber, 40, Ann-street

Reid & Cavert, fustian and calico manufacturers, and wholesale dealers in cotton yarn, muslin, &c. 31, High-street

Reid, James, woollendraper, 22, Bridge-street

Reilly & co. vinegar and mead manufacturers, 25, Hercules-lane

Richards, Thomas, saddler, 77, Ann-street

Rider, Job, clock and watchmaker, and optician, 27, High-street

Rippett, George, boot and shoemaker, 154, North-street

Ritchie, William, ship-builder, 17, Fore-plantation

Ritchie, Hugh, ship builder, Chichester-quay

Ritchie, James, smith, 16, Back-lane

Roberts, John, grocer, 12, Mill-street

Robinson, John, hatter, 29, Ann-street

Robinson, A & C. haberdashers, 65, High-street

Robinson, Thomas, portrait painter, 30, Castle-street

Robinson, Samuel, grocery and seed shop, 73, Waring-street

Rogers, Esther, & Sisters, haberdashers, 12, High-street

Roney, James, tavern keeper, 4 Leg's-lane

Ross, John, cambric manufacturer, 19, Castle-street

Rowan, Henry & co. distillers, 35, Barrack-street

Rowan, James & co. druggists, Castle-street

Russell, James, watchmaker, 4, Waring-street

Russell & Woods, cotton spinners, and manufacturers, 22, Brown-street

Rutherford, Ann, inn and stable-keeper 30, Ann-street

Rutherford, Jordan & co. muslin manufacturers, 192, North-street.

S

Scott, James, grocer, 59, Ann-street

Scott, Benjamin, painter and glazier, 8, Chapel-lane

Scott, Alexander, merchant, Lime-kiln-dock

Seed, Richard, soap-boiler and tallow-chandler, 42, High-street

Seeds & Bailie, merchants, 1, Weigh-house-lane

Setten, Joseph, sea-bread baker, 45, Waring-street

Sergison, Edward, victualler, 146, North-street

Shaw, Deborah, haberdasher, 3, Castle-street

Shaw, James, saddler, 23, Prince's-street

Shaw, John, coal factor, 2, Hanover-quay, & 41, Fore-plantation

Sheriff, Joseph, boot and shoemaker, 6, North-street

Simms, Robert & William, merchants, Chichester-quay

Simms & M'Intyre, printers and booksellers, 25, High-street

Simms, Henry, grocer, 18, Waring-street

Simpson, John, grocer and spirit dealer, 2, North-street

Sinclair, William, merchant, 20, Donegall-place

Sinclair, Alexander, woollendraper, 17, High-street

Sinclair, John, grocer, 89, Ann-street

Sinclair, John, grocer, 12, Church-lane

Skelton, William, tavern-keeper, Long-lane

Sloan, George, grocer, 190, North-street

Sloan, David & co. fustian and calico manufacturers, 25, Smith-field

Sloan, John & James, smiths, 83, North-street

Sloan, Samuel, stone-cutter, 29, John-street

Smith, J. Galt, woollendraper and broker, 26, High-street

Smith, Samuel, wholesale & retail, grocer and tobacco and snuff manufacturer, 37, North-street

Smylie, James, stone cutter, Talbot-street

Smyth, Mary, haberdasher, 66, High-street

Smyth & Lyons, printers, 71, High-street

Smyth, Samuel, reed maker, 81, Peter's-hill

Smyth, Hugh, hosier, 18, Smith-field

Snell, George & co. muslin manufacturers, 52, Peter's-hill

Snell, Thomas, cabinet-maker, 34, North-street

Soden, Martin, navy agent, 34, Prince's-street

Spence, David, haberdasher, 8, High-street

Spencer, William, boot and shoemaker, 57, Castle-street

Spring, Edward, cork-cutter, 15, Hercules-lane

Standfield, James, grocer, 95, High-street

Standfield, Charles, grocer and spirit dealer, High-street

Steel, Matthew, soap-boiler and tallow chandler, 10, Castle-street

Sterling, Hugh, turner, 4, Talbot-street

Stevenson, William & Joseph, merchants, York-street

Stewart, John, china and glass-seller, 22, Corn-market

Stewart, Samuel, copper-smith, 14, North-street

Stewart, Alexander, grocer and spirit dealer, 33, North-street

Stitt, James, woollen and linen-draper, 30, High-street

Stitt, Robert, grocer, 78, Ann-street

Storey, James, bookseller, 202, North-street

Stormont, William, painter and glazier, 26, North-street

Suffern, John, tobacconist, 191, North-street

Sweeny & Lynn, merchants, Calendar-street.

T

Talbot, Richard, tailor, 1, Waring-street

Taylor, William, cabinet-maker, 21, Donegall-street

Taylor, Hugh, boot and shoemaker, High-street

Telfair, Robert, merchant, 6, Ann-street

Templeton, Matthew, boot and shoemaker, 32, Berry-street

Tennent & M'Connell, wine and spirit merchants, 63, Waring-street

Tennent, Knox & co. merchants, 11, Waring-street

Thompson, William, linen merchant, Donegall-square, west

Thompson, Andrew, wine and spirit merchant, 54, High-street

Thompson, George, grocer, 13, Talbot-street

Thompson, Henry, merchant-taylor, 32, Castle-street

Thompson, Samuel, grocer, 97, Ann-street

Thompson, John, engraver, 8, Pottinger's-entry

Thomson, Charles & William, grocers, High-street

Trail, Robert, woollendraper, 8, Bridge-street

36

Trail, John, haberdasher and grocer, 55, Ann-street

Tucker, Eliza Houlden, haberdasher, 23, Bridge-street

Tucker, William, muslin manufacturer and commission warehouse, Castle-lane

Turnly & Batt, merchants, Ann-street

Turnly, Alexander, linen merchant, 48, Ann-street.

V

Vance, John, wholesale English woollen warehouse, 7, Waring-street

Vance, John & co. Irish woollen warehouse

Vint, John, inn-keeper, 141, North-street.

W

Walker, William, grocer, tobacco and snuff manufacturer, Corn-market

Wallace, Lyle and Whittle, flour and grain merchants, 3, Chichester-quay

Wason, Hugh & co. merchants, Byrt's-entry, High-street

Ward, Thomas & co. booksellers, 19, High-street

Ward, Michael, tavern-keeper, 4, Corn-market

Ward, James, bookbinder 2, Wilson's-court

Ward, Jeremiah, grocer and spirit dealer, 67, Mill-street

Warnick & M'Clelland, haberdashers, 7, Castle-street

Watson, John, carver, gilder and print seller, 12, Castle-street

Watt, William, cotton manufacturer, 71, Waring-street

Wharton, James, grocer 1, Church-street

Wharton, John, grocer and cooper, 82, Hercules-lane

Whinnery, Thomas, post master, and agent for London newspapers, 6, Church-street

White, Thomas, cotton machine-maker, 7, Thomas-street

White, John, muslin manufacturer, West-street

Whittle, James & John, wholesale woollendrapers, 66, Waring-street

Whitla & Armstrong, woollendrapers, 21, High-street

Wilson, Mary, haberdasher and milliner, 62, High-street

Wilson, Hugh & Son, merchants, 152, North-street

Wilson, Thomas, inn-keeper, Donegall-arms, Castle-street

Wilson, Joseph, hatter, 103, Ann-street

Wilson, John, junior, grocer, 135, North-street

Wilson, William, white-smith, 2, Long-lane

Wilson, Robert, spirit dealer, 31, Waring-street

Wilson, Hugh, cooper, 49, Waring-street

Wills, Eliza. milliner, 32, High-street

Williamson, James, landsurveyor and draughtsman, Lilliput-hill, near Belfast

Williamson, Thomas, grocer, 66, Ann-street

Winnington, James, book-binder, 12, Chapel-lane

Woods, David, hardware and toy-warehouse, 2, Skipper's-lane

Woods, Phillip, cap maker, 17, Hercules-lane

Workman, Rose, mantua-maker, Hill-street, off Waring-street

Wright, John, coach-maker, 22, Prince's-street

Wright, Ludford, copper-smith, 35, Ann-street.

Y

Yates, John, china-seller, 42, Church-lane

Young, James, cabinet-maker, 9, Church-lane

ATTORNIES.

Arthur, James, Arthur-street
Cranston, William, Arthur-street
Echlin, D. Moore, Arthur-street
Gordon & Hamilton, Arthur-street
Montgomery, Robert, Prince's-street
M'Guckin, James, South-parade
Ramsay & Garret, Rosemary-lane
Stewart, T. Ludford, Castle-yard
Waring, Richard, South-parade
Whitla, Francis, Donegall-street
Wright, Joseph, Rosemary-lane.

BARRISTERS.

Dobbs, Richard, esq.
Orr, Alexander, esq.

CLERGY.

Acheson, Rev. Robert, director of Ballymacarret school
Bristow, Rev. William, Vicar general of Down and Connor
Bruce, Rev. William, D.D. Principal of the Belfast Academy
Cassidy, Rev. Peter, Berry-street
Dobbs, Rev. Robert, Donegall-street
Drummond, Rev. William, Mount Collyer Academy
Hanna, Rev. Samuel, Rosemary-lane
Holmes, Rev. William, Waring-street
Nicholson, Rev. John, Academy-row
O'Donnell, Rev. Hugh, Hercules-lane
Brown, William, Evangelical minister, North-street

39

Dinnen, John, Methodist minister

Lougheed, William, ditto

Main, Charles, ditto.

PHYSICIANS.

Those marked thus (*) are Practitioners in Midwifery.

* Ferguson, Samuel, 15, Mill-street

Forsythe, James, 28, Donegall-street

* Haliday, William, 2, Donegall-place

* M'Donnell, James, 8, Donegall-place

* M'Donnell, Alex. M.D. & surgeon, 22, Waring-street,

* M'Gee, Robert, 9, North-street

* Stephenson, S. M. 70, Waring-street

* Thomson, Samuel Smith, 26, High-street

SURGEONS, &c.

Anderson, William, druggist and apothecary, 47, High-street

* Bankhead, John, surgeon and apothecary, 92, High-street

Bell, James, surgeon, 65, Waring-street

* Brady, Nicholas, surgeon and apothecary, 31, High-street

Bryson, Samuel, surgeon and apothecary, 50, High-street

* Campbell, John, surgeon and apothecary, 68, Donegall-street

* Marshall, Andrew, surgeon, chemist and apothecary, 51, High-street

Montgomery, James, apothecary, 77, High-street

M'Clelland, Richard, surgeon and druggist, 41, High-street

40

* M'Cluney, Robert, surgeon and apothecary, 55, Castle-
street
* Rowan, James, surgeon and apothecary, 62, Castle-
street

LONDON AND LIVERPOOL NEW TRADERS.

At present under the Direction of a Committee of the Owners, viz.

Hugh Crawford,	R. Hyndman,	F. M'Cracken,
Narcis. Batt,	W. Tennent,	A. Guy, Assistant.

Office....lower end of Waring-street.

Hibernia, *Caughey*
Saint Patrick, *Campbell*
Draper, *M'Donnell*
Venus, *Montgomery*
Jane, *Taylor*
Kelly, *Pendleton*
Neptune, *Davidson*
Minerva, *Busby.*

To Bristol, &c.
Diana, *M'Kibbin*
Swallow, *M'Niece.*

To Dublin, &c.
Haslett and Montgomery, agents.

Dispatch, sloop, *Dobbin*
Hawk, brig, *Agnew.*

DUBLIN TRADERS.

CLOTWORTHY BIRNIE, AGENT.

Johns, brig, *Downey*
Trial, cutter, *Curran.*

MR. LANGTRY'S TRADERS.

From this to London, Liverpool, &c.

Cunningham Boyle, *Bell*
Commerce, *Kearney*
Factor, *Conway*
Lagan, *M'Connell*
Ceres, *Martin*
Aurora, *Fitzsimons*
William, *M'Crea*
Fame, *Smith*
Fanny, *Courtney*
Experiment, *Gregg*

GLASGOW TRADERS.

Mr. Robert Gemmill, Agent.

Betseys, sloop, *Galbraith*
Margaret and Nancy, sloop, *M'Indoe*
Roberts, sloop, *Bisset.*

*** *It is humbly requested, that the Inhabitants of Belfast will be so kind as to communicate to us any addition, or correction, which may tend to render a Directory of Belfast extensively useful; and, that all the Householders, who may remove from one street or number, to another, may submit to the trouble of informing us of such removal.*

Smyth & Lyons, printers and publishers.

BELFAST

DIRECTORY,

FOR 1808;

OR,

A LIST OF THE NAMES AND PLACES

OF

THE MERCHANTS, TRADERS, &c.

Alphabetically arranged;

ALSO THE PRINCIPAL PROFESSIONAL CHARACTERS,
AND PUBLIC INSTITUTIONS.

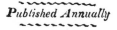

Published Annually

PRINTED AND PUBLISHED BY SMYTH & LYONS,
High-street.

TO THE PUBLIC.

The great and important improvements made by our active and judicious Police, since the first arrangement of the Belfast Directory, though they have somewhat retarded the publication, highly tend to promote its utility......the names of several streets having been changed, some new ones projected, and the numbers entirely altered, required as strict inspection as on its first compilation.

We expect its present form will be found convenient and in general correct......comprising such improvements and alterations as have taken place since the first of February.

In every department we have invariably attended to alphabetical order......in that of the Mercantile and Trading, we were in some instances at a loss to discriminate and affix the appropriate title of business, according to the person's being less or more extensive in trade......conscious of impartial intention, we hope to be excused for any such error, and shall gadly receive any hint that may tend to obviate future objections.

We have also given a list of the professional Gentlemen, and the principal public Institutions, &c. of the town, alphabetically arranged.

The following are the principal alterations, &c.

Cow-lane, *now Mary-street*........Fore-plantation, *James'-street*......Buttler's-row, *Gordon-street*.....Back-plantation, *Grattan-street*......Hercules-lane, *Hercules-street*......Back-of-the-River, *Bank-lane*......South parade, *Donegall-square*......from the head of Donegall-street past the Barracks......*Queen-street*.......from the Bridge-end to the Custom-house-corner, *Custom-house-quay.*

*** *We, in the most earnest manner, request that any removals or alterations, during the year, may be notified to us, prior to the 10th November next.*

215, *High-street.*   *SMYTH & LYONS.*

BELFAST DIRECTORY,

FOR 1808.

MERCHANTS, TRADERS, &c.

A

ADAIR, Simon, cooper, 50, Waring-street

Agnew, James, ladies' shoemaker, 17, Skipper's-lane

Alexander, John & co. merchants, Belfast-mills

Alexander, Samuel, tanner, 78, North-street

Alexander, John, hotel and car-men's-inn-keeper, 11, Peter's-hill

Alexander, John, junior, cotton-spinner and manufacturer, cotton-court, Waring-street

Alexander, Robert, saddler, 5, Waring-street

Allen, Ann & Mary, haberdashers and milliners, 16, Castle street

Allen, Mary Ann, haberdasher, 8, Corn-market

Allen, William, boot and shoemaker, 82, High-street

Anderson, Drummond, editor of the Commercial Chronicle, 5, Wilson's-court

Anderson, James, watch and clockmaker, 2, Waring-street

Anderson, Martin, spirit dealer, 24, Ann-street

Andrews, Samuel, merchant-tailor, 8, Marlbro'-street

Appleton, David, hosier and tavern-keeper, 121 & 122, Ann street

Archbold, Edward C. wholesale woollen and hosiery warehouse, 21, Church-street

Archer, Samuel, bookseller and printer, 21, High-street

Armstrong, David S. woollen and carpet-warehouse, 20, High-street

Armstrong, John, breeches-maker, 61, Castle-street

Armstrong, Robert, cotton-manufacturer, 56, Smith-field

Asylum for the Blind, 30, High-street

Atkinson, Eliza, haberdasher, 102, High-street

Atkins, James, coach and house painter, 29, Prince's-street

Auchinleck, William, senior, public notary, and tobacco-broker, 185, North-street.

B

Bailie, Robert, merchant, 1, Upper Chichester-street

Bailie, James, merchant, 190, North-street

Bailie, John, boot and shoemaker, 40, Ann street

Bailie, Robert, hat manufacturer, 5, Bridge-street

Baird, James, confectioner, 10, Rosemary-lane

Baker, James, muslin manufacturer, 9, Talbot street

Barkley, James, tavern and ordinary-keeper, 3, Sugar-house-entry

Barnett, Andrew John, merchant, 65, High-street

Barnett, John, tanner, 49, Castle street

Barr, Alexander, woollendraper, 117, High-street

Batt, Narcissus & Robert, merchants, Calendar-street

Belfast Glass Company, 80, Peter's-hill

Belfast Porter Brewry, Smith-field

Belfast Repository, 116, Ann-street

Bell, John & co. muslin manufacturers, Margaret-street

Bell, John, brewer, 55, Hercules street

Bell & Kennedy, wholesale printed calico, and linen-warehouse, 62, Waring-street

Bell & Haughton, hardware merchants, 79, High-street

Bell, William, woollendraper, 18, Bridge street

Bell, Alexander, woollendraper, 2, Bridge street

Bell, Isaac, senior, upholsterer, 101, High street

Bell, Isaac, junior, upholsterer, 21, Bank-buildings

Bell, William, dyer, 8, Mill-field

Bell, John, pawnbroker, 28, Smith-field

Bell & Harvey, nursery and seedsmen, 12, Church-lane

Bell & M'Call, cabinet-makers, 6, Pottinger's-entry

Bell, William, cork-cutter, 12, Rosemary-lane

Berwick, William & co. merchants, 1, North-street

Bigger, David, merchant, 5, High-street

Birnie, Clotworthy, shipbroker, public notary and auctioneer, 1, Chichester-quay

Black, Matthew, woollendraper, 7, Bridge street

Black, Alexander, grocer, 23, High-street

Blackader, John, boot and shoemaker, 20, North-street

Blackwell, Alexander, linendraper, 38, High-street

Blackwell, William James, wholesale haberdasher, 1, Donegall-street

Blackwell, William, cabinet maker, 61, Donegall-street

Blackwood, Charles, victualler, 18, Corn-market

Blackwood, Thomas, victualler, 13, Corn-market

Blair, Andrew, hosiery warehouse, 12, Bridge-street

Blow, Ward & co. paper manufacturers, 113, Ann-street

Boomer, James, cotton spinner and manufacturer, 18, Mill-street

Boswell, John, watchmaker, 24, Pottinger's-entry

Boyd, Nathaniel, tavern keeper, 37, Berry street

Bourdot, John Baptist, ladies' and gentlemen's hair dresser and perfumer, 42, Castle street

Bowden, James, soap-boiler and tallow chandler, 74, Ann-street

Bradford, James, merchant, 9, Store-lane

Bradford, George & Benjamin, merchants, 46, High street

Broadley, Ben. & co. cotton wool and tow card manufacturers, 30, Smith-field

Brown, Samuel, merchant, Calendar-street

Brown, David, painter and glazier, 50, Mill street

Brown, John, anchor smith and coach-maker, 21, Back-lane

Brown, John, patten and ladies' shoemaker, 67, Hercules street

Brown, Samuel, hairdresser and perfumer, 59, Castle-street

Brown, Andrew, grocer, 12, Ann-street

Bryson, John, grocer, 55, Ann-street

Bullen, John, nursery and seedsman, 100, Ann-street

Buchannan, Walter, merchant, 4, Chichester-quay

Bunting & Ash, boarding school for young ladies, 67, Donegall-street

Burke, Robert, feather and skin merchant, 33, Hercules-street

Burke, Patrick, feather warehouse, 19, Skipper's lane

Burns William, merchant-tailor, 11, Bridge-street

Burns, Robert, hairdresser and peruke maker, 15, Skipper's-lane

Burnside, John, furniture cotton warehouse, 15, Donegall street

Byres, William & co. muslin manufacturers, 22, Donegall street.

C

Callwell, Robert, merchant, Upper Chichester street

Campbell, Samuel & James, merchants, 196, North-street

Campbell, Hugh, muslin manufacturer, Brown street

Campbell, Christopher, inn and livery stable keeper, 102, Ann street

Campbell, Charles, boot and shoemaker, 10, Mill street

Campbell, William, rope and twine manufacturer, 44, North street

Campbell & Smylie, stone and marble yard, 23, Waring-street

Carey & Cooper, china and earthen warehouse, Lime-kiln-dock

Carmichael, Robert, woollendraper, 9, High-street

Carrol, William, victualler, William-street, south

Carson, James, grocer, spirit and wine merchant, 1, Corn-market

Carson, James, timber-merchant, 48, Ann-street

Carson, Thomas, spirit dealer, 14, Hercules-street

Carson, William, fustian warehouse, 5, Hercules-street

Caughey, Isabella, slop shop, 10, Chichester-quay

Caughey, James, ship chandlery shop, 64, High-street

Cavan, John, grocer, 2, High-street

Chambers, Brice & co. wine and spirit merchants, 17, Ann-street

Christian, Thomas, cart-maker, 11, Malbro' street

Clarke, Sampson, hat manufacturer, 66, Castle street

Clarke, John, cabinet maker, 9, Rosemary-lane

Clawson & Hill, grocers and tobacconists, 26, Rosemary-lane

Cleland, Jane, china glass and staffordshire warehouse 17, Castle-street

Coats, Victor, founder and starch manufacturer, Lagan, Ballymacarret

Cochran, George, fancy furniture ware-room, 16, Smithfield

Cochran, Ernest, tailor, 1, Wilson's-court

Colville, James, woollendraper, 15, Bridge-street

Colville, John, woollendraper, 19, Bridge street

Cooney, John, victualler, 9, Corn-market

Cooper, David, haberdasher, 77, High-street

Cowan, Jane & Ellen, grocers, 81, Ann-street

Craig, Samuel, wine and spirit merchant, 5, Marlbro'-street

Crawford, Hugh, merchant, 26, Donegall-street

Crawford, Walter, iron merchant, 10, Donegall-street

Crawford, Ann, grocer, 14, Church lane

Crawford, James, cabinet-maker, 20, Waring-street

Crossen, James & co. muslin manufacturers, Brown-street

Cuddy, John, glazier, paint, oil and glass store, 20, Church lane

Cuddy, William, plumber, 13, Marlbro'-street

Cumming, Mary, haberdasher, 28, Bridge-street

Cummin, Samuel, leather seller, 168, North street

Cunningham, John, merchant, 95, High street

Cunningham, John & Thomas, spirit merchants, 78, Mill-street

Cunningham, John, hosier, 13, Donegall-street.

D

Daniel, Stephen, dyer, 39, North-street

Davis, Robert, merchant, 12, Chichester-quay

Davis, Joy, hat manufacturer, 24, Bridge-street

Davis, Patrick, glazier, paint, oil and glass store, 19, North-street

Davis, William, inn-keeper and horse repository, 125, North-street

Davison, Gawn, tobacconist and grocer, 83, Ann-street

Davison, William, merchant, 106, High-street

Davidson, John, haberdasher, 4, Bridge-street

Dawson, William, boot and shoemaker, 60, High-street

Delap, Robert, broker, 7, Chichester-quay

Demsey, Matthew, pawnbroker, 5, Pottinger's-entry

Demsey, James, shoemaker, 93, Ann-street

Dickson, Simon, boot and shoemaker, 24, North-street

Dickson, William, cotton manufacturer, 10, Carrick-hill

Doherty, John, printer and bookseller, 30, Bridge-street

Doherty, Edward, spirit dealer, 93, Ann-street

Donaldson, Jane, haberdasher, 108, High-street

Donaldson, John, block-maker and pump-borer, 67, High-street

Donnelly, John, spirit dealer, 53, Smith-field

Douglass, William & co. merchants, 6, Marlbro'-street

Drummond, Rose, circulating library, 12, Castle-street

Duff, John, box-book-keeper to the theatre, 31, Lodge-lane

Duffield, Samuel, carmen's-inn-keeper, 118, North-street

Dunlop, James & Robert, coal-factors, 38, Prince's-street

Dyke, R. W. crayon and miniature painter, and drawing master, 75, Mill-street.

E

Edwards, Hugh & Benjamin, glass manufacturers and founders, Ballymacarret

Ekenhead, Thomas, rope and sail manufacturer, 56, Ann-street

Elliot, John, linen merchant, 12, Donegall-street

English, Thomas, dyer, 12, Mill-field

F

Fallon, Margaret, grocer and spirit dealer, 18, Church-lane

Faloon, James, spirit dealer and tavern keeper, 3, Hanover-quay

Faloon, William, spirit dealer, 31, Waring-street

Ferguson, R & E. haberdashers, 123, High-street

Ferguson & Elliot, wine and spirit merchants, 57, Hercules-street

Ferguson, William & John, haberdashers, 50, High-street

Ferguson, William, tailor, Legg's-lane

Fetherston, Ann & sisters, haberdashers, 33, Castle-street

Finlay, Robert, cotton spinner and manufacturer, 15, Mill-field

Finlay, Alexander, soap-boiler and tallow-chandler, 56, High-street

Finlay, Usher, slop shop, 61, High-street

Fitzsimons, Samuel, carpenter, 31, Waring-street

Fitzsimons, Allice, haberdasher, 118, High-street

Fitzsimons, James, tailor, High-street

Fletcher, Thomas, soap-boiler and tallow-chandler, 157, North-street

Flowers, M. Ann, haberdasher, 11, Castle-street

Forcade, John, saddler, 64, Castle-street

Fox, George, grocer, 183, North-street

Frazier, Joseph, grocer, 12, Patrick-street

Frazier, James, carmen's-inn-keeper, 75, Peter's-hill

B

Freebairn, John, stocking-frame-maker, 65, Patrick-street

Fulton, Nathaniel, soap-boiler and tallow-chandler, 3, North-street.

G

Gamble, Arthur, merchant, 17, North-street

Gamble, Robert, merchant, 201, North-street

Gamble, William, spirit dealer, 35, Waring-street

Gardner, Henry L. watchmaker and dentist, successor to J. Rider, 27, High-street

Gardner, Wills, joiner, 17, Prince's-street

Gardner, John, gun-smith, 9, Rosemary-lane

Gardner, Arthur, grocer, 55, High-street

Gemmill, Robert, muslin manufacturer, 65, Donegall-street

Getty, Robert, merchant, 16, North-street

Getty & Armstrong, hardware merchants, 207, North-street

Getty, John, cabinet maker, 63, Donegall-street

Gibson, Samuel, merchant, 20, Donegall-street

Gibson, Samuel & co. brewers, 185, North-street

Gibson & Simms, wholesale printed calico and muslin warehouse, 5, Donegall-street

Gihon, Jane, haberdasher, 6, Castle-street

Gihon, Robert, merchant, 84, High-street

Gillespie, William, haberdasher, 32, North-street

Gillet, Henry, tavern-keeper, Belfast Hotel, 22, Arthur-street

Gillies, John, merchant, 6, Custom-house-quay

Gilmore, Joseph, baker, 20, Ann-street

Glancey, James, staymaker, 18, Rosemary-lane

Gold, John, bookbinder, 49, Mustard-street

Gordon, James, cotton manufacturer, Brown-street

Gordon, John, grocer, 202, North-street

Gordon, Hugh, engraver, 24, Church-lane

Gowdy, James, hairdresser, 179, North-street

Graham, Campbell, wine and spirit merchant, 118, Ann-street

Graham, Hugh, linen draper, 5, C. Peter's-hill

Graham, Thomas, copper and tin smith, 74, High-street

Graham, John, block-maker and pump-borer, 66, High-street

Grainger, James, brick-layer, 96, Ann-street

Grainger, Mary, grocer, 95, Ann-street

Grainger, William, baker, 28, Mill-street

Gray, John, hosier, 47, High-street

Gray, William, boot and shoemaker, 49, High-street

Greenlaw, Robert, merchant, Church-street

Greenlaw & Ware, agents for the new established London and Liverpool Traders, 40, Waring-street

Greer, James, boot and shoemaker, 76, High-street

Greer, Samuel, grocer, 193, North-street

Greer, William, sen. weavers' mechanic, 67, North-street

Greer, William, junior, weavers' mechanic, 120, North-street

Greg & Blacker, merchants, 50, Ann-street

Greg & Boyd, vitriol works, Ballymacarret

Grimshaw, Robert, merchant, 58, Waring-street

Grogan, John, linen-merchant, Donegall-square

Grogan, Robert, linen-merchant, Henry-ville

57

Groves, David, glover and skinner, 31, Castle-street

Groves, William, glover and skinner, 30, Church-lane.

H.

Hadskis, Ann, grocer, 199, North-street

Hadskis, Susanna, haberdasher, 37, Rosemary-lane

Hall, John Joshua, watchmaker, 33, High-street

Halliday, Mary, haberdasher and milliner, 110, High-street

Hamilton, Robert, tailor, 18, Wilson's-court

Hannay M'William, & co. cotton yarn warehouse, 53, Donegall-street

Hamill, Ann, grocer, 96, High-street

Hamill, John, provision merchant, 53, Waring-street

Harper, James, master joiner, 26, Mill-street

Harper, Thomas, tailor, 183, North-street

Harrison, Mary, haberdasher, 26, Bridge-street

Hart, Robert, glazier, 36, Church-lane

Henan, Hugh, umbrella-maker, 98, Ann-street

Henderson, Robert, joiner, Brown-street

Henesey, David, sen. fancy-chair maker, 11, Rosemary-lane

Henesey, George, fancy-chair maker and furniture painter, 12, Rosemary-lane

Heron, Thomas, merchant, 51, Ann-street

Heron, John, merchant, 15, Ann-street

Herdman, John, brewer, 60, Ann-street

Herdman, James, tanner and currier, 9, Mill-street

Hewett, Samuel, wine and spirit merchant, grocer and tobacco manufacturer, 32, Ann-street

Hibner, Ellis, victualler, South-William-street

Higgins, John, machine maker, 108, Mill-field

Higginson, William, inn-keeper and ordinary, 24, Done-gall-street

Hill, Edward, grocer, 198, North-street

Hodgson, Robert and John, bookbinders and stationers, 4, High-street

Hodgson, Thomas, saddler, 63, Hercules-street

Hoey, Samuel, cooper, 74, Hercules-street

Holmes & Barklie, merchants, 16, Ann-street

Horner, Anthony, muslin manufacturer, 26, Wine-tavern-street

How, John & Thomas, muslin manufacturers, 19, Church-street

Huddleston, Francis & co. muslin manufacturers, 21, Joy's-court

Hudson, Christopher, tanner, 147, North-street

Hudson, David, carmen's-inn-keeper, 121, North-street

Hughes's & Moore, provision merchants, 17, adjoining the Weigh-house

Hughes, Thomas, grocer, 8, North-street

Hughes, Ann, haberdashery and toyshop, 32, Rose-mary-lane

Hunter, William, grocer, 2, Donegall-street

Hutcheson, John, haberdasher, 203, North-street

Hutton, William, hardware and toyshop, 52, High-street

Hyndman, Robert, snuff and tobacco manufacturer, 120, High-street

Hyndman, James, public notary and auctioneer, 17, Donegall-street.

I

Jack, Samuel, victualler, 159, North-street

Jamison, William, inn-keeper, 29, North-street

Jamison, James, tanner, 103, North-street

Janson, Henry M. painter and glazier, 47, Waring-street

Johnson & Fisher, wholesale woollendrapers, 34, Rosemary-lane

Johnson, William & co. wholesale woollendrapers and haberdashers, 78, Donegall-street

Johnson & Halliday, wholesale woollendrapers and haberdashers, 78, Donegall-street

Johnson, Young & co. wholesale haberdashery warehouse, 77, Donegall-street

Johnston, James, spirit merchant and grocer, 189, North street

Johnston, John, grocer, 110, Ann-street

Johnston, William, baker, 16, Mill-street

Johnston, Robert, haberdasher, 24, Mill-street

Jordan, Simon, cabinet-maker, 39, Smith-field

Joy, Holmes & Tomb, merchants, Wine-cellar-entry

Joy, James, and co. cotton manufacturers, Wine-cellar-entry

Joyce, Charles Valentine, & co. wine and spirit merchants, 4, Waring-street

Ireland, Frances, haberdasher, 127, High-street

Ireland, M. & E. haberdashers, 126, High street

Ireland, John, livery stables, 126, High-street

Ireland, Thomas, cotton spinner and manufacturer, 19, Mill-field

Irwin, William, cooper, 28, Waring-street.

K

Kearney, James, china and delf-seller, 87, Ann-street

Kearns, Hugh, spirit dealer, 76, Ann-street

Kelso, Paul, grocer and spirit dealer, 166, North-street

Keenan, John, painter and glazier, 31, Berry-street

Kennedy, James Trail & co. merchants, 23, Leg's-lane

Kennedy John, junior, merchant, Waring-street

Kennedy, John, baker, 87, Hercules-street

Kennedy, Sarah, haberdasher, 104, High-street

Kennedy, Alexander, woollendraper, 7, Bridge-street

Kennedy, Daniel, cutler, 20, Chapel-lane

Kennedy, Charles, grocer, 200, North-street

Kennedy, Samuel, tavern and inn-keeper, 3, Waring-street

Kenning, Thomas, muslin warehouse, 30, Castle-street

Kerr, Daniel, tavern-keeper and ordinary, 104, Ann-street

Kilbee, James & co. Old Sugar House, 3, Rosemary lane

...................., public notary and master in chancery

Kirk, Hugh, public notary, master in chancery, auctioneer and printer, 2, Fountain-street

Kirkpatrick, John, merchant, 42, Waring-street

Kirkpatrick, Samuel, grocer, 19, Church-lane

Kirkpatrick, Thomas, soap-boiler and tallow chandler, 43, High-street

Knox, John, watchmaker, 14, High-street

Knox, John, boot and shoemaker, 2, Castle-street.

Knox, Robert, shoemaker, 35, High-street

L

Lamont & Ireland, boarding-school for young ladies, 6, Donegall-street

Lamont, Ann, earthen-ware shop, 8, Skippers-lane

Langtry, George, merchant, 22, Waring-street

Law, James, baker, 93, High-street

Law, Samuel, tanner, 112, North-street

Law, James, tanner, 110, North-street

Law, Andrew, brazier, 11, Hercules-street

Lawrence, James, perfumer and hairdresser,, 107, Ann-street

Letham, Robert, linen merchant, 60, Donegall-street

Letham, John, merchant, Calendar-street

Leathem, Robert, confectioner, 59, Waring-street

Lepper, George, watchmaker, 10, Bridge-street

Lepper, Francis, watchmaker and dentist, 67, Castle-street

Lepper, Charles, grocer and spirit merchant, 197, North-street

Lewes, Robert, boot and shoemaker, 29, High-street

Lewis, George, haberdasher, 128, High-street

Linden, Matthew, confectioner, 34, Castle-street

Lindsay, Edward, nursery and seedsman, 4, Donegall-street

Linn, Catherine, haberdasher and milliner, 1, Castle-street

Linn, Jane, haberdasher and milliner, 122, High-street

Linn, Patrick, inn-keeper, white cross, 1, Castle-street

Linn, Robert & co. soap-boilers and tallow-chandlers, 88, High-street

Linn, David, grocer and spirit dealer, 60, Barrack-street

Lowry, Robert, wine and spirit merchant, 16, Corn-market

Luke, John & son, woollendrapers, 31, Bridge-street

Luke, James, pottery-shop, 204, North-street

Lyle & Riddle, hardware merchants, 107, High-street.

M

Macartney, John, agent for the General Insurance Company, 2, Custom-house-quay

Mackay, Alexander, editor of the Belfast News-Letter, 13, Bridge-street

Magee, Jane, haberdasher, 12, North-street

Magee, William, bookseller and stationer, 23, Bridge-street

Magee, Con. inn-keeper, 129, North-street

Magee, James, tavern and stable keeper, 75, Ann-street

Maphei, William & co. salt works, Ballymacarret

Marshall, Hugh, tailor, 7, Pottinger's entry

Martin, Jane, tavern and stable keeper, 30, North-street

Martin, John & co. merchants, 14, Ann-street

Martin, George, hardware merchant, 25, Bridge-street

Martin, William and James, saddlers and curriers, 39, Castle-street

Martins & Park, merchants, 10, Church-lane

Matthews, James & Robert, merchants, 68, Ann-street

Matthews, John, boot and shoemaker, 8, castle street

Matthews, Robert, boot and shoemaker, 10, Castle street

Matthews, Robert, haberdasher, 21, Ann-street

May, Richard, grocer, wine and spirit merchant, 90, Ann-street

Meneally, James, grocer, 58, Barrack-street

Miles, Mary, baby linen and corsit shop, 2, Rosemary-lane

Milford, John & co. cotton manufacturers and spinners, Winetavern-street

Millar, Mary, haberdasher, 96, Ann-street

Millen, George, wholesale printed calico and haberdashery warehouse, 11, Donegall-street

Miller, George, rope and twine manufacturer, 164, North-street

Miller, Samuel, starch manufacturer, and provision merchant, 36, Donegall-street

Miniss, Charles, peruke maker, 47, Ann-street

Mollyneaux, Joseph, baker and starch manufacturer, 8, Church-street

Montgomery, Jane & H. straw-bonnet manufacturers, 40, Prince's-street

Montgomery, Tennent & co. New Sugar House, 8, Waring street

Montgomerys, Staples & co. merchants, 2 Calender-street

Montgomery, George, coast-broker, 9, Chichester-quay

Montgomery, Josias, saddler, 124, High-street

Montgomery, Gawn, woollendraper, 45, High-street

Montgomery, Henry, haberdasher, 14, Bridge-street

Montgomery, John, grocer, 23, Prince's street

Mooney, William, surveyor and measurer, 41, Hercules-street

Moore, Thomas, rope and twine manufacturer, 70, High-street

Moore, Eliza, haberdasher, 30, North-street

Moreland, Arthur, victualler, 14, Cornmarket

Morgan, John, grocer, 152, North-street

Morrow, William, tavern-keeper, 5, Hanover-quay

Mountford, John, cotton spinner and manufacturer, York-street

Mountford, Hugh, smith, 84, Ann-street

Muckle, Robert, wool and tow card maker, 170, North-street

Mulholland, Roger, architect, 12, Castle-street

Mulrea, William, woollendraper, 16, Bridge-street

Munfoad, E. & M. haberdashers, 103, High-street

Murdoch, Richard, smith, 103, Ann-street

Murphy, William, grocer, 22, Ann-street

Murray, Timothy, soap-boiler and tallow-chandler, 178, North-street

Mussenden, Charles, boot and shoemaker, 43, Ann-street

Myres, George, china, glass and earthen warehouse, 81, High-street.

Mc.

M'Adam James, hardware merchant, 113, High-street

M'Adam, George, hardware and toy merchant, 114, High-street

M'Adam, Marshall & co. wholesale druggists, and oil and colour merchants, 41, High-street

M'Auley & Kenley, haberdashers, 68, Castle-street

M'Burney, James, tailor, 6, Crown-entry

M'Bride, Ursula, haberdasher, 13, High-street

M'Bride, John, grocer, 172, North-street

M'Cabe, Edmond & Thomas, gilders and chair-makers, 50, Talbot-street

M'Cammon, John, tanner and currier, 52, Mill-street

M'Cappin, William, provision merchant, Cotton-court, Waring-street

M'Cartney, James, smith, 1, Marlbro'-street

M'Clarnon, Pat. provision merchant, 14, Hercules-street

M'Clean, Adam, woollendraper, 111, High-street

M'Clean, Samuel & Andrew, wine and spirit merchants, 1, Sugar-house-entry

M'Clean & Hull's house-furnishing, ironmongery and hardware-house, 22, Bank-buildings

M'Clean, William, wine and spirit merchant, 192, North-street

M'Clean, Charles, silk dyer, 5, Mill-street

M'Cleery, James, merchant, 191, North-street

M'Clement, David, merchant and grocer, 79, Ann-street

M'Clure, Bailie & Whitla, merchants, Donegall-quay

M'Clure, William, merchant, 8, Donegall-street

M'Clure, John, grocer, 57, Barrack-street

M'Clure, Robert, boot and shoemaker, 28, North-street

M'Clure, Joseph, boot and shoemaker, 187, North-street

M'Comb, Thomas, timber merchant and salt stores, 41 & 43, Waring-street

M'Connell, John, merchant, 9, Ann-street

M'Connell & co. wholesale haberdashery warehouse, 14, Donegall-street

M'Connell, Alexander, earthenware-house, 59, High-street

M'Connell, William, farming-utensil-maker, 5, Smith-field

M'Cosh & Irwin, merchants, 6, Rosemary-lane

......................., tobacco-manufacturers, 24, Rosemary-lane

M'Cord, Andrew, grocer, 5, North-street

M'Coubery, Robert, grocer, 93, Ann-street

M'Cracken, Margaret & co. muslin manufacturers, 39, Waring-street

M'Cracken, R. Ann, haberdasher, 35, Castle-street

M'Cracken, John & co. cotton spinners, Donegall-street

M'Cracken, Francis, merchant, 38, Waring-street, and rope and sail manufacturer, 1, James'-street

M'Cracken, William, cotton manufacturer, 35, Castle-street

M'Credie, John, saddler, 43, Castle-street

M'Crum, John, fustian, cotton, and muslin manufacturer, 11, Skipper's-lane

M'Culloch, John, linen merchant, 162, North-street

M'Cully, William, publican and stable keeper, 27, Ann-street

M'Cune, Samuel, sea-bread baker, 7, Mary-street

M'Donnell, Thomas, merchant, 13, North-street

M'Fadden, Archibald, baker, 18, Ann-street

M'Garragh, Alexander, grocer, 77, Ann-street

M'Ilroy, Archibald, muslin manufacturer, 16, Patrick-street

M'Kean, James, grocer, 23, Ann-street

M'Kee, William, woollendraper, 1, Bridge-street

M'Kee, Robert, confectioner, 36, Ann-street

M'Kee, John, confectioner, 62, Castle-street

M'Kibbin, Hugh & co. tanners and glue manufacturers, 22, Mill-street

M'Kibbin, Beck & co. wholesale haberdashers, 3, Donegall-street

M'Kittrick, William, Haberdasher, 46, High-street

M'Lister, John, soap-boiler and tallow-chandler, 3 Ann-street

M'Master, James, merchant, 42, North-street

M'Millan, Neill, muslin manufacturer, Queen-street

M'Mullan, John, tavern keeper, 3, Pottinger's-entry

M'Neice, William, reed-maker, Peter's-hill

M'Neill, Margaret, haberdasher and milliner, 132, High-street

M'Nerney, & co. hosiery warehouse, 29, Bridge-street

M'Pherson, James, peruke maker and hair dresser, 40, Church-lane

M'Queelin, J. Davys, spirit dealer and tavern keeper, 10, Chichester-quay

M'Tier, James, baker, 76, North-street

M'Whinney, Thomas, grocer, 67, Ann-street

M'William, John & co. cotton-yarn warehouse, 68, Donegall-street.

N

Nagle, Francis, spirit merchant, 14, North-street

Napier, William, brewer, Bank-lane

Neill, Robert, watchmaker, 1, High-street

Neilson, Ann, haberdasher, 99, High-street

Neilson, Robert & co. linen merchants, Fountain-street

Neilson, William, watchmaker, 205, North-street

New Rope walk Company, 6, Chichester-quay

New Brewry Company, 1, Chapel-lane

Newsam, William & co. wholesale haberdashers, 6, Donegall-street

Newsam, William, tobacco and snuff manufacturer, 119, Ann-street

Nicholl, Andrew, boot and shoemaker, Church-lane

Nicholl, William, cooper, 3, Skipper's-lane.

O

O'Connor, Anthony, distributor of stamps, 72, Donegall-street

O'Donnell, Charles, master in chancery, 12, Arthur-street

O'Neill, Thomas & co. printed calico, muslin and cotton yarn warehouse, 74, Donegall-street

Orr, James, merchant, Donegall-square.

P

Palmer, John, spirit dealer and tavern keeper, 4, Hanover-quay

Park, James, saddler, 18, North-street

Park, James, fustian and cotton manufacturer, 9, West-street

Parker, John, stone cutter, 17, Smith-field

Patrick, Hugh, baker, 10, Berry-street

Patrick, William, haberdasher, 6, Bridge-street

Patterson J. E. & M. haberdashers, 98, High-street

Patterson, Robert & John, hardware merchants, 112, High-street

Patterson, Joseph, brick-layer, 62, Ann-street

Patton & M'Alister, factors, White-linen-hall

Patton, Isaac, wholesale haberdasher, 124, High-street

Patton, Frances, haberdasher, 18, High-street

Patton, Barbara, haberdasher, 121, High-street

Peirry, Samuel, boot and shoemaker, 91, High-street

Phelps, William, broker and general merchant, 3, Lime-kiln-dock

Pinkerton, Andrew, merchant, 22, Bridge-street

Porter, Edward, cutler, 19, Corn-market

Potter, Mary, grocer, 25, Prince's-street.

Q

Quinn, Arthur, boot and shoemaker, 6, High-street

Quaile, Roger, inn and stable keeper, 28, Prince's-street.

R

Radcliff & Munce, wholesale woollendrapers, 3, Bridge-street

Ramsay, Esther, grocer, 29, Castle-street

Rea, John, merchant-tailor, 28, High-street

Reid, Thomas, spirit merchant, Leg's-lane

Reid, William, plumber, 49, Ann-street

Reid & Cavert, fustian and calico manufacturers, and wholesale dealers in cotton yarn, muslin, &c. 32, High-street

Reid, James, woollendraper, 20, Bridge-street

Reilly & co. vinegar and mead manufacturers, 30, Hercules-street

Richards, Thomas, saddler, 88, Ann-street

Rippett, George, boot and shoemaker, 161, North-street

Ritchie, William, ship-builder, 4, James'-street

Ritchie, James, smith, 24, Back-lane

Roberts, John, grocer, 12, Mill-street

Robinson, Ann, haberdasher, 37, Ann-street

Robinson, John, hatter, 37, Ann-street

Robinson, A. & C. haberdashers, 109, High-street

Robinson, Thomas, portrait painter, 37, Castle-street

Robinson, Samuel, grocery and seed shop, 72, Waring-street

Robinson, ———, boarding-school for young ladies, 28, Donegall-street

Rogers, Esther, & Sisters, haberdashers, 12, High-street

Rogers, Malcolm, glover and breeches-maker, 120, Ann-street

Roney, James, tavern keeper, Leg's-lane

Ross, John, cambric manufacturer, 28, Castle-street

Rowan, Henry & co. distillers, Barrack-street

Rowan, James & co. druggists, 1, Corn-market

Russell, James, watchmaker, 6, Waring-street

Rutherford, Ann, inn and stable-keeper, 38, Ann-street

Rutherford, Jordan & co. muslin manufacturers, 197, North-street.

S

Scott, James, grocer, 71, Ann-street

Scott, Benjamin, painter and glazier, 8, Chapel-lane

Scott, Alexander, merchant, Lime-kiln-dock

Sedgwick, Mary & Allice, milliners, 11, Corn-market

Seed, Richard, soap-boiler and tallow-chandler, and commission merchant, 42, High-street

Seeds & Bailie, merchants, 1, Weigh-house-lane

Sergison, Edward, victualler, 154, North-street

Service, John & co. wine and spirit merchants, 17, Corn-market

Setten, Joseph, sea-bread baker, 44, Waring-street

Shanaghau, Daniel, writer and conveyancer, Ann-street

Shaw, Deborah, haberdasher, 4, Castle-street

Shaw, James, saddler, 65, Ann-street

Shaw, John, coal factor, 1, Custom-house-quay, and 26, James'-street

Sheriff, Joseph, boot and shoemaker, 124, Ann-street

Simms, Robert & William, merchants, 8, Chichester-quay

c 2

Simms & M'Intyre, printers and booksellers, 24, High-street

Simpson, John, grocer and spirit dealer, 2, North-street

Sinclair Alexander, woollendraper, 17 High-street

Sinclair, John, grocer, 11, Church-lane

Skelton, William, tavern-keeper, 2, Long-lane

Sloan, John, public notary, Discount-office, Bridge-street

Sloan, George, grocer, 194, North-street

Sloan, David & co. fustian and calico manufacturers, 36, Smith-field

Sloan, John & James, smiths, 85, North-street

Sloan, Samuel, stone-cutter, John-street

Smith, J. Galt, woollendraper and broker, 26, High-street

Smith, Samuel, wholesale and retail, grocer and tobacco and snuff manufacturer, 41, North-street

Smylie, John, clerk to the Commissioners of Police, 73, High-street

Smyth & Lyons, printers, 115, High-street

Smyth, Samuel, reed maker, 82, Peter's hill

Smyth, Hugh, hosier, 28, Smith-field

Snell, George & co. muslin manufacturers, 57, Peter's-hill

Snell, Thomas, cabinet maker, 38, North-street

Soden, Martin, navy agent, 37, Prince's street

Spence, David, haberdasher, 8, High-street

Spencer, William, boot and shoemaker, 65, Castle-street

Spellane, Timothy, spirit dealer and tavern-keeper, 1, Ann-street

Spring, Edward, cork-cutter, Hercules-street

Standfield, Margaret, haberdasher, 131, High street

Standfield, James, grocer, 133, High-street

Standfield, Charles, grocer and spirit dealer, 54, High-street

Steel, Matthew, soap-boiler and tallow chandler, 15, Castle street

Stephenson, Samuel, grocer, 39, High-street

Sterling & Faulkner, cotton-yarn warehouse, 111, Ann-street

Sterling, Hugh, turner, 4, Talbot-street

Stevenson, Jane, haberdasher, 21, Bridge-street

Stevenson, William & Joseph, merchants, York-street

Stewart, Robert & co. spirit merchants, 20, Rosemary-lane

Stewart, John, china and glass-seller, 20, Corn-market

Stewart, Samuel, copper-smith, 15, North-street

Stewart, Alexander, grocer and spirit dealer, 36, North-street

Stitt, N. & J. milliners, 35, Ann-street

Stitt, James, woollen and linen-draper, 30, High-street

Stitt, Robert, grocer, 89, Ann-street

Storey, James, bookseller, 206, North-street

Stormont, William, painter and glazier, 26, North-street

Suffern, John, tobacconist, 195, North-street

Sweeny, Campbell, merchant, Calendar-street.

T

Talbot, Richard, tailor 1, Waring-street

Taylor, William, cabinet-maker, 21, Donegall-street

Taylor, Hugh, boot and shoemaker, 80, High street

Telfair, Robert, merchant, 11, Ann street

Templeton, Matthew, boot and shoemaker, 22, Church-lane

Tennent & M'Connell, wine and spirit merchants, 63, Waring-street

Tennent, Knox & co. merchants, 11, Waring-street

Thompson, William, linen merchant, Donegall-square, west

Thompson, Andrew, wine and spirit merchant, 97, High-street

Thompson, George, grocer, 13, Talbot-street

Thompson, Henry, merchant-tailor, 40, Castle-street

Thompson, Samuel, grocer, 112, Ann-street

Thompson, John, engraver and seal-cutter, 105, Ann-street

Thompson, Charles & William, grocers, 57, High-street

Thonboe, Michael, Danish and Swedish ship agent and foreign linguist, 2, Fountain-street

Toler, Charles, haberdasher, 129, High-street

Trail, Robert, woollendraper, 9, Bridge-street

Trail, John, haberdasher and grocer, 66, Ann-street

Trimble Robert, grocer and spirit stores, 84, Peter's-hill

Tucker, William, muslin manufacturer and commission-warehouse, Castle-lane

Turnly & Batt, merchants, 52, Ann-street

Turnly, Alexander, linen merchant, 59, Ann-street.

V

Vance, John, wholesale English woollen warehouse, 7, Waring-street

Vance, John & co. Irish woollen warehouse 7, Waring-street

Vecchio, Charles Del. carver and gilder, 23, Bank-buildings

Vint, Elizabeth, inn-keeper, 151, North-street.

W

Walker, William, grocer, tobacco and snuff manufacturer, 12, Corn-market

Wallace, Lyle & Whittle, flour and grain merchants, 4, Chichester-quay

Wallace, Thomas, woollendraper, 116, High-street

Wason, Hugh & co. merchants, Byrt's-entry, High-street

Ward, Thomas & co. booksellers and stationers, 19, High-street

Ward, James, bookbinder, 2, Wilson's-court

Ward, Jeremiah, grocer and spirit dealer, 79, Mill-street

Ward, Michael, tavern-keeper, 4, Corn-market

Ware, Susanna, boarding-school for young ladies, 49, Bank-lane

Warnick, Martha, haberdasher, 9, Castle-street

Watt, William, cotton manufacturer, 71, Waring-street

Wharton, James, grocer, 14, Church-street

Wharton, John, grocer and cooper, 91, Hercules-street

Whinnery, Thomas, post-master and agent for London newspapers, 23, Church-street

White, John, muslin manufacturer, 24, Mill-field

Whittle, James & John, wholesale woollen drapers, 66, ware-house-lane, Waring-street

Wilson, Mary, haberdasher and milliner, 105, High-street

Wilson, Hugh & Son, merchants, 163, North-street

Wilson, Thomas, inn-keeper, Donegall-arms, 5, Castle-street

Wilson, John, junior, grocer, 36, North-street

Wilson, Hugh, cooper, 48, Waring-street

Wilson, William, white-smith, Long-lane

Wilson, William, umbrella and parasol manufacturer, 35, North-street

Wills, Elizabeth, milliner, 31, High-street

Williamson, James, land surveyor and draughtsman, Lilliput-hill, near Belfast

Williamson, Thomas, grocer, 66, Ann-street

Winnington, James, book-binder, 12, Chapel-lane

Woods, Mary, hardware and toy-warehouse, 2, Skipper's-lane

Workman, Rose, mantua-maker, Hill-street, off Waring-street

Wright, John, coach-maker, 23, Prince's-street

Wright, Ludford, copper-smith, 42, Ann-street.

Y

Yates, John, china-seller, 47, Church-lane

Young, James, woollen and Manchester, warehouse, 31, Rosemary-lane

Young, James, cabinet-maker, 9, Church-lane

Young, James, book-binder and copper-plate printer, High-street.

———

✱✱✱ In some of the foregoing, and many of the following, the houses are not numbered....particularly Donegall-place, and some in bye-places.

PROFESSIONAL CHARACTERS.

ATTORNIES.

Arthur, James, Donegall-square

Cranston, William, 15, Arthur-street

Echlin, D. Moore, 58, Ann-street

Montgomery, Robert, 40, Prince's-street

M'Guckin, James, Donegall-square

Ramsay & Garret, 17, Rosemary-lane

Stewart, T. Ludford, 58, Castle-yard, Castle-street

Waring, Richard, Donegall-square

Whitla, Francis, 27, Donegall-street.

Wright, Joseph, 7, Rosemary-lane.

BARRISTERS.

Crombie, William, Belfast, and 2, North-King-street, Dublin

Dobbs, Richard, Belfast, and Castle-dobbs

Joy, Henry, Belfast, and Temple-street, Dublin

Orr, Robert, Belfast, and 76, Marlbro'-street, Dublin.

CLERGY.

Acheson, Rev. Robert, of the Belfast Classical and Commercial School, 17, Church-lane

Bristow, Rev. William, Vicar general of Down and Connor, 27, Donegall-street

Bruce, Rev. William, D. D. Principal of the Belfast Academy, Donegall-street

Cassidy, Rev. Peter, 16, Berry-street

Dobbs, Rev. Robert, 27, Talbot-street

77

Drummond, Rev. William, Mount Collyer Academy

Hanna, Rev. Samuel, 4, Rosemary-lane

Holmes, Rev. William, 6, Church-street

Nicholson, Rev. John, 3, Academy-row

O'Donnell, Rev. Hugh, 33, Hercules-street

Brown, William, Evangelical minister, 185, North-street

Crook, William, Methodist minister, Donegall-square, east

Dinnen, John, Methodist minister, Donegall-square, east

Mayne, Charles, Methodist minister Donegall-square, east.

MASTERS IN CHANCERY.

Messrs. James Kilbee, Rosemary-lane.......Hugh Kirk,
Fountain-street.....Charles O'Donnell, Arthur-street....
H, Waterson, Ann-street.

MEDICAL STAFF.

Comins William, surgeon, and deputy inspector-general
of hospitals, Arthur street

Purdon, Henry, staff-surgeon, Donegall-square

Stafford, William, district surgeon, Donegall-street.

Stewart, John, assistant staff-surgeon, Hercules-street.

NOTARIES PUBLIC.

Messrs. William Auchinleck, North-street....C. Birnie,
Chichester-quay.......P. Connor, Arthur-street.......J.
Hyndman, Donegall-street......J. Kilbee, Rosemary-
lane.....Hugh Kirk, Fountain-street.....J Sloan, Discount-office.

PHYSICIANS.

Drennan, William, 1, Donegall-square, south

Forsythe, James, 28, Donegall-street

Haliday, William, 2, Donegall-place

* M‘Donnell, James, Donegall-place

* M‘Donnell, Alex. M. D. & surgeon, 23, Waring-street

* M‘Gee, Robert, 11, North-street

* Stephenson, S. M. 70, Waring-street

Stott, William, 3, Castle-street

* Thompson, Samuel, S. 23, Donegall-street.

SURGEONS, &c.

Anderson, William, druggist and apothecary, 86, High-street

* Bankhead, John, surgeon and apothecary, William-street, south

Bell, James, surgeon, 65, Waring-street

* Brady, Nicholas, surgeon and apothecary, 34, Ann-street

Bryson, Samuel, apothecary, 90, High-street

* Campbell, John, surgeon and apothecary, 76, Donegall-street

* Marshall, Andrew, surgeon chemist and apothecary, 94, High-street

Montgomery, James apothecary, 119, High-street

* M‘Cluney, Robert, surgeon and apothecary, 63, Castle-street

* Rowan, James, surgeon and apothecary, 70, Castle-street

Those marked thus (*) are practitioners in Midwifery.

PUBLIC INSTITUTIONS, &c.

Academy, Rev. W. Bruce, principal, 30, Donegall-street.

Asylum for the Blind, 36, High-street.

Belfast Classical and Commercial School, conducted by the Rev. Robert Acheson and Mr. Samuel Lyons, 17, Church-lane.

Belfast Weekly or Sunday-school, off Waring-street, for the Education of such Persons as are not likely to have the means or opportunity of otherwise obtaining any.

Car, Cart and Waggon stands, are opposite the weigh-house; the old Church-yard-wall, so far as Church-lane....penalty for standing any other place ten shillings.

Chamber of Commerce, 17, Donegall-street.....council, Robert Bradshaw, esq. president....Narcissus Batt. esq. vice-president.....Robert Callwell, secretary.....Messrs. Hugh Crawford....George Langtry.....George Joy.... Robert Getty.....Robert Davis....William Stevenson.... John Gillies.....Cunning. Greg....Campbell Sweeny.... John Cunningham....Robert Hyndman....Richard Staples....William Tennent.

Constable, high, John Smyth, esq. Donegall-place.

Constables appointed at Court-leet....Messrs. George Lepper, Bridge-street....James' Crawford, Waring-street..... Hugh M‘Kibbin, Mill-street....James Moore, William-street, south.....Stephen Daniel, North-street.

Coroner, Mr. James Stewart, 98, Hercules-street.

Corporation of the borough of Belfast....The Most Noble the Marquis of Donegall, Lord of the Castle of Belfast ....Edward May, junior, esq. Sovereign....Hon. C. Skeffington, constable of the Castle....Twelve Burgesses.... Rt. Hon. Earl of Massareene...Rev. W. Bristow...Rev.

G. Macartney.....Ar. Chichester, esq.....E. D. Wilson, esq....Geo. Bristow, esq....Rev. Dr. S. Cupples...Lord S. Chichester....Sir Wm. Kirk....Edward May, senior, esq. ....T. L. Stewart, esq....Rev. Rich. Wolseley....Messrs. William Byrt, town clerk; John Smylie, deputy town clerk....Richard Moore and James Alderdice, serjeants at mace.

Corporation for preserving and improving the port and harbour of Belfast.....office, 2, Custom-house-quay..... Members, The Most Noble the Marquis of Donegall, Lord of the Castle of Belfast....Rt. Hon. John Foster.... Sir John Newport, baronet....Messrs. John Turnly.... Narcissus Batt....Hugh Crawford...John Cunningham... Hugh, Montgomery....Val. Jones....Robert Bradshaw.., Cunningham Greg....George Langtry....Robert Hyndman...George Joy...Richard Staples...meet every Wednesday....ballast-master, Mr. John Macartney....keeper of the graving-dock, Mr. Jackson Clark.....harbourmaster, south-side, Mr. John Shaw....ditto, north-side, Mr. Thomas Griffith....deputy ballast-masters...Messrs. William Mattear, and William Mackenzie.

Customhouse, corner of Hanover quay.....officers...... Hon. C. Skeffington, collector.....H. A. S. Harvey, esq. port-surveyor.....George Black, esq. landwaiter.....F. Coulson, esq. landwaiter....Edward May, junior, esq. storekeeper....T. B. Martin, guaging surveyor....Christopher Salmon, pro-collector....Isaac Thompson, deputy comptroler....James M'Key, permit clerk, and clerk of the cheque.

Discount-office, 27, Bridge-street....days of discounting, Mondays, Wednesdays and Fridays....members.... Messrs. Gilbert M'Ilveen, Belfast....Robert Bradshaw, ditto....George Joy, ditto....Henry Joy Tomb, ditto.... John Robinson, ditto....John Hamilton, Ballyalloly....

Hugh Montgomery, Benvarden....John Thompson, Jennymount....John Stewart, Lakefield.

Dispensary and Fever Hospital, 32, West-street....committee....Rev. Wm. Bristow....Rev. Robert Dobbs....Rev. William Holmes.....Val. Jones, esq. secretary.....William Clarke, esq. treasurer......James M'Donnell and Samuel S. Thompson, physicians....Robert M'Cluney and Andrew Marshall, surgeons.....James Murray, apothecary.

Exchange....Days of business....Mondays, and Wednesdays, at 12 o'clock, and Fridays, at 11 o'clock.

Excise-office....William-street, south....Mr. Peter Quin, pro-collector.

Fire-engines, 27, William-street....the following persons have keys of the house....the Church-warden....John Graham, 66, High-street....Robert Smith, head inspector of Police, 3, Wine-tavern-street.

Fire Insurance offices....Dublin Insurance office....Messrs. Samuel & Andrew M'Clean, agents.

The Commercial Insurance Company of Dublin....Mr. J. Ward, agent.

British and Irish united Fire Insurance co. London and Dame-street, Dublin....Messrs. N. & R. Batt, agents.

The Corporation of the Royal Exchange Assurance Company of London....Mr. Greenlaw, agent.

Galvanic society, is held in a room off Waring-street.

General Insurance office, 2, Custom-house-quay.

Linenhall, white, Donegall-square.

Linenhall, brown, Donegall-street.

Literary Society meets monthly, has for its object Polite Literature, Science, and antiquities.....Rev. William Drummond, president.

Lying in-Hospital, 44, Donegall-street.

Magistrates, resident in Belfast....Rt. Hon. C. Skeffington, Castle-street......Rev. William Bristow, Talbot-street....Thos. Andrews, esq. Donegall-street.....George Bristow, esq. Donegall-square, south....George Joy, esq. Donegall-place....A. Chichester, esq. Donegall-place....William Clarke, esq. Donegall-place....T. Thompson, esq. Bank-buildings....Rev. R. Wolseley, Donegall-square......Gilbert M'Ilveen, esq. Donegall-place.....Edward May, junior, esq. Donegall-place.....W. Fox, esq. Fox-lodge, Town-major, attends daily.

Mail-coach from Belfast to Dublin, sets off every morning at half past 9 o'clock from the Donegall-arms, carries one outside and four inside passengers....fare, inside, £1 16 3½....outside, £1 2 9.

Market for Meat, Fish, Meal, Potatoes and green Vegetables, entrances from Castle-lane, Arthur and William-streets.

Medical Library.....committee. ...Samuel S. Thompson, M. D. president....William Haliday, M. D......Robert M'Gee, M.D.....Robert M'Cluney, surgeon....Andrew Marshall, surgeon, secretary and treasurer.

Pipe-water Committee....Messrs. William Clarke....William Newsam....Joseph Stevenson....A. J. Barnett....James M'Cleery.....sit every Saturday....John Smylie, clerk.

Police Commissioners*....N. Batt, esq....V. Jones, esq....R. Bradshaw, esq....H. Crawford, esq....G. Joy, esq....W. Clarke, esq...A. J. Barnett, esq....G. M'Ilveen, esq. ... C. Greg, esq....W. Stevenson, esq....the Sovereign, for the time being, and Burgesses......John Smylie, clerk.

---

* Here two members are to be appointed.

Police Committee....Messrs. J. Stevenson.....J. Smyth....
T. Whinnery...H. Johnson...H. Wilson...C. Hudson...
J. Gregg...G. Langtry....R. Callwell....A. Stewart...C.
Sweeny...W. Thompson....W. Magee....R. Hyndman
...A. M'Clean.....J. Douglas....R. Getty....J. M'Adam...
W. Newsam....J. M'Cammon....R. Simms.

Poorhouse and Infirmary, upper end of Donegall-street...
committee...Rev. W. Bristow...Rev. R. Dobbs...Rev. S.
Smyth...Rev. W. Holmes...Rev. S. Hanna....Messrs.
W. Clarke....R. Stevenson....S. Gibson.....T. M'Donnell....D. Bigger....W. Newsam...J. M'Cleery.

Post-office, Church-street...Mr. T. Whinnery, Postmaster.

Public Day School, 27, Berry-street....established and
conducted by Ladies....the Children receive a gratui-
tous education.

Sedan-chairs....stands are at the dead-wall, west side of
Donegall-place, and the Exchange....fare, $6\frac{1}{2}d$. for a
set-down until twelve o'clock....1s. after twelve, and
1s. 6d. after one o'clock in the morning....if detained
more than fifteen minutes, an additional sixpence.

Society for Promoting Knowledge, is held in the White-
linen-hall....Rev. W. Bruce, D. D. president....S. M.
Stephenson, M.D. vice president....T. M'Donnell, sec.
and treasurer....J. Sloan, librarian.

Society for Acquiring Knowledge, is held at 13, Talbot-
street....James Dunlop, treasurer; George Thompson,
librarian.

Sovereign of Belfast, Edward May, junior, esq. Donegall-
place.

Stamp-office, Donegall-street, A. O'Connor, esq. distributor.

Town-major, William Fox, esq. Fox-lodge.

Town-clerk, W. Byrt, J. Smylie, deputy T. C.

Weigh-house, lower end of Waring-street.

LONDON AND LIVERPOOL NEW TRADERS,

GREENLAW AND WARE, AGENTS.

Saint Patrick, *George M'Kibbin, master*
Venus, *Samuel Montgomery*
Vine, *Alexander M'Donnell*
Draper,
Kelly, *Nathaniel Pendleton*
Neptune, *Alexander Davidson*
Jane, *Hugh Busby.*

G. LANGTRY'S REGULAR TRADERS,

From this to London, Liverpool and Bristol.

Factor, *James Conway, master*
Aurora, *George Fitzsimons*
Graces, *James Caughey*
Lagan, *Alexander M'Connell*
Cunningham Boyle, *Thomas Bell*
Fanny, *Edward Courtenay*
Minerva, *James Kean*
Commerce, *James Kearney*
Ceres, *William Martin*
Swift, *William M'Neice*
Swallow, *Charles Courtenay*
Experiment, *John Gregg.*

TO DUBLIN, &C.

GEORGE MONTGOMERY, AGENT.

Dispatch, sloop, *Rankin*
Hawk, brig, *Dobbin.*

DUBLIN TRADERS.

CLOTWORTHY BIRNIE, AGENT.

Johns, *Downey*

Tryal, cutter, *Curran*

~~~~~~~

GLASGOW TRADERS.

ROBERT GEMMILL, AGENT.

Betsies, sloop, *Rose*

Margaret and Nancy, sloop, *Galbraith*

Roberts, sloop, *Bisset.*

We are gratefully indebted to respectable gentlemen for the following additions and corrections, and for some valuable hints of future improvement.

CLERGYMEN.

Groves, Edward, Church-street

Smith, Samuel, Donegall-street

Wolseley, Richard, Donegall-square

Allen, Susanna & Sisters, boarding school for young ladies, 13, Wilson's-court

Bryson, Alexander, soap-boiler and tallow-chandler, 60, Waring-street

Bunting, Edward, organist and musician, 38, Waring-street

Bunting, John, musician, 67, Donegall-street

Cooney, Courtney, victualler, 6, Ann-street

Cramsie & Connor, merchants, William-street

86

Fabrini, Gaetano, drawing-master, Arthur-street

Ferguson, John S. linen merchant and factor, Donegall-place

Hull, Thomas, dancing-master, and master of ceremonies of the Belfast Assembly, 11 & 12, Ann-street

Hutcheson, John & co. wholesale woollen and fustian warehouse, 203, North-street

Kain & Maitland, cabinet-makers, 7, Ann-street

Luke, Robert, merchant, 16, North-street

May, Thomas, muslin manufacturer, Arthur-street

Miller, James, auctioneer, 12, Crown-entry

Mitchell, Thomas, architect and builder, West-street

M'Key, James, permit officer and clerk of the cheque

Norris, Edward, sculptor and marble-stone mason, 24, Pottinger's-entry

Ritchie, John, ship-builder, Bridge-end

Sedgwick, John, cotton-yarn merchant, 19, West-street

Sinclair, John, merchant, Donegall-place

Smith, Robert, head inspector of Police, 3, Wine-tavern-street....Burn, Thomas, deputy ditto.

Stewart, Alexander, linen-merchant, Arthur-street

Thompson, Thomas, ladies shoemaker, 97, Ann-street

Ware, William, organist and musician, 49, Bank-lane

Watson, John, drawing-master, Rosevale....orders taken at 33, Castle-street

Whitla Geo. & Val. merchants, Donegall-quay

Whitla, George, jun. & co. muslin manufacturers, 10, Donegall-street

Young, James, painter, 17, Charlemont-street

*In consequence of the following changes or removals....*DELE

Andrews, merchant-tailor, Marlbro'-street

Crombie, barrister

Workman, mantua-maker, Hill-street

Grainger, Ann-street, for Mary *read* Catherine

☞ *The Publishers of this infantile Directory, are aware that it is not yet so complete as could be wished, and earnestly solicit the intelligent to communicate any addition or correction tending to render it more extensively useful......They again, in the most respectful, though earnest manner, request that any person, in business, who may have been omitted, or whose name, number, or address may be wrong, will inform them of the same; and also, that any alteration or removal may be notified prior to the 10th of November next.*

February, 1808.

Smyth & Lyons, printers and publishers.